Using the UNIX System

Using the UNIX System

Richard Gauthier

RLG Corporation

Reston Publishing Company, Inc.
A Prentice-Hall Company
Reston, Virginia

Library of Congress Cataloging in Publication Data

Gauthier, Richard L.
    Using the UNIX system.

    Bibliography
    Includes index.
    1. UNIX (Computer system)   I. Title
QA76.7.G37   001.64   81-10571
ISBN 0-8359-8164-9   AACR2
    0-8359-8162-2 (pbk)

Copyright © 1981 by
Reston Publishing Company, Inc.
A Prentice-Hall Company
Reston, Virginia

10 9 8 7 6 5 4

Printed in the United States of America

CONTENTS

ACKNOWLEDGMENTS

I am indebted to many of my colleagues and friends who painstakingly read the manuscript, "Using The UNIX System", and made suggestions for improvements in addition to correcting typographical errors.

In particular, I would like to thank Jack Waugh and Dan Porges for their contribution to chapter 9 on "System Administration"; Wendel Yale, Stu McDonald and other members of the RLG Corporation technical staff for their critical review and ideas for examples; ATEX, UNIDOT, and Santa Cruz Operations for their critical reading of the manuscript; Bob McClure and Kent Harris of UNIDOT for their assistance in helping me typeset the book; and to all the others that I may have overlooked, but who contributed to its completion.

This book was typeset using Don Knuth's TeX system running under UNIX on the ONYX C8002.

Type used in this book is from the family of computer modern type fonts designed by Don Knuth with METAFONT. Final output was produced on the Alphatype CRS at BNR INC. and the Stanford Computer Science Department. Special thanks to David Fuchs at Stanford and Patrick Milligan at BNR INC. for their assistance and patience during the final stages of the phototypesetting process.

TeX, a system for technical text. Copyright 1979 by the American Mathematical Society.

To my family - Pat and Darrin - who made sure that everything I thought was obvious, was.

PREFACE

"USING THE UNIX* SYSTEM" has been written for people with some knowledge of computer sciences, but with no specific knowledge of the UNIX system. However, this does not exclude those who are already using the UNIX system. They will find that many options exist that are rarely used, but extremely valuable.

The UNIX system presented in this book is based on version 7.

How to read this book

Chapters 2,3, and 4 are designed for the novice who is just about to learn the UNIX system or has just started. These three chapters provide the foundation necessary to understand the basics of the UNIX system and continue on to the following chapters of this book.

The basic items covered in these chapters are:

Logging in and out of the UNIX system

Setting your password

The UNIX command format

Creating and maintaining files

Getting around in the file system

Use of some basic UNIX commands

---

*Unix is a trademark of Bell Laboratories

Chapter 6 introduces the basic functions and capabilities of the Shell program such as:

I/O direction

Pipes and filters

Background commands

Metacharacters

Chapter 8 continues with some of the more advanced capabilities of the shell program such as:

Shell files

Shell arguments

Nesting shell files

Chapters 5 and 7 provide a description of many of the more frequently used commands. They have been placed in sections pertaining to their function.

The sections included are:

Manipulation of files and directories (chapter 5)

Communications (chapter 7.1)

Information Handling (chapter 7.2)

Running Programs (chapter 7.3)

Status Inquiries (chapter 7.4)

Terminal Handling (chapter 7.5)

The last chapter, chapter 9, covers the duties of the system administrator and should be read last. This covers those functions necessary to control who uses the system, backup and recovery of the system, the file system, and the use of those commands dedicated to the maintenance of the system in general.

The appendices cover such things as the answers to questions, some of the UNIX system error messages, and a brief summary of all the commands defined in this book. They do not cover all of the options that are available, but only the most frequently used ones.

It would be impossible in any reasonably sized book to cover all of the ways in which one could use these commands. I have tried to describe the ones that you would be most likely to use with the idea in mind that they will give you clues as to how you might extend your knowledge to more sophisticated usages.

1. Introduction

UNIX is more than just an operating system for 16 and 32 bit computers. It has become a trademark for a family of software written with unusual simplicity that can be easily directed at a large number of applications such as office automation, database management, communications, etc. In addition, there exists a wealth of software tools that can be used to generate new applications.

Although the UNIX system was designed for program development, it has proven to be an ideal system for software applications.

The UNIX system offers many features for program development and applications such as:

o A hierarchical file system

o Compatible file, device and interprocess I/O

o Asynchronous processing

o Command language interpreter

o Over 100 subsystems and utilities

o A variety of languages including Fortran 77,
  Fortran VI, Pascal, Basic, and C

While all of these features are nice, the real advantage is that they can be made available on a new computer within a very short time frame. This again is because of the inherent portability aspects of the UNIX system.

The time required to move the UNIX system to a new computer is not only less expensive, but is only a fraction of what would be required to rewrite the vast amounts of existing software applications.

Although the UNIX system was designed and implemented first on the PDP-11 computer, one of its strong points has been its "portability". This combined with the large number of application programs has made it a target of most modern mini and micro computers. At this point in time, the UNIX system has been implemented on many systems, some of which are the PDP-11 family, the DEC VAX, IBM Series/1, Zilog Z8000, Amdahl 470, Univac 1108, Perkin Elmer/Interdata and Univac V77.

The first UNIX system became operational in February of 1971. Currently there are over 2500 installations with more being added each day. UNIX is the standard interactive system at almost every major university in the world and is becoming increasingly common in most of the commercial world.

Rapid advances and changes are now occurring in electronic technology and state-of-the-art computer and communication architecture. These changes, combined with end-user demand for turn-key small scale systems are one of the driving demands for the UNIX system.

Many commercial corporations are planning their future product strategies around the UNIX system. They believe that the UNIX system is part of a wave of the future in generating new computing applications.

2. Getting Started

There are two things you must have before getting started. The first is a login name. This is usually selected by you and provided by the system administrator. Your login name is generally your first name, nickname, or your initials. Without it you will not be able to use the UNIX system. The second is a terminal. The UNIX system is capable of dealing with a wide variety of terminals. If you have a choice, find one that has an easy keyboard to use. The set up of your terminal is also important. For the time being this is best done by the system administrator. If you have any problems report them to the administrator. Later we will discuss some of the duties of the administrator.

Now assuming we have a login name and a terminal we can get started. Once the terminal is turned on and connected to the UNIX system, "login:" will appear on your terminal. You then enter your login name provided by the system administrator and the UNIX system will respond with a prompt sign "$". This is an indication that the UNIX system has accepted your login name and is ready to do your bidding.

Example:

```
UNIX  ->   login:
user  ->   dick<r>              remember you must depress
                                the return key "<r>"
```

3

```
UNIX  ->   $                    UNIX is ready, you are in the
                                system and ready to go
```

One of the first things to remember is that you must always depress the return key(sometimes known as the carriage return key) after entering any command or responding to a UNIX command. We will indicate that a return key is required by the symbol "<r>". The UNIX response to your input that is accepted is always a "$" unless you are the superuser (more on this later). If the input was not correct, UNIX will respond either with a brief message(see appendix A) or with a "?".

Example:

UNIX response to an illegal login name:

```
UNIX  ->   login:
user  ->   dack<r>                login name should be "dick"
UNIX  ->   passwd:                Asking for a password
```

The UNIX system will not let you know that the login name is illegal, thus making it harder for someone to make a guess at a real login name. In this case nothing you enter will allow you to log into the UNIX system. Any input by you will result in the "login:" command being typed again.

```
UNIX  ->   login incorrect
      ->   login:
```

At this point you can try again. The system will continue to do this until you enter a correct login name.

2.1. Setting and Using a Password

When you are first assigned a login name you do not as yet have a password. The system administrator does not set it. Once you have successfully logged into the system you can then set your own password. This is done by entering the command "passwd<r>". The passwd you issue must be longer then 6 characters or if shorter it must be complex (i.e., use special and non printing characters).

Example:

We will assume that "dick" is logged into the system.

```
user   ->   passwd<r>
UNIX   ->   Changing password for dick
       ->   New password:
user   ->                          enter password, but not
                                    echo'd
UNIX   ->   Retype new password:
user   ->                          enter password, but not
                                    echo'd
UNIX   ->   $                      indicates password was ac-
                                    cepted
```

In this example it was the first time the password had been set. This is indicated by the UNIX command "New password:". In each case (entering original password and retyping it) the system does not display the characters typed by you. This is to help insure that no one can see what it is.

Now let's change an existing password:

Example:

```
user   ->   passwd<r>
UNIX   ->   changing password for dick
       ->   Old password:
user   ->                          enter password, but no echo
UNIX   ->   New password:
user   ->                          enter new password, but no
                                    echo
UNIX   ->   Retype new password:
user   ->                          enter new password, but no
                                    echo
```

We have now entered an original password and then changed it. In each case we made no mistakes. However if we did make a mistake, the system would have issued a diagnostic. Following is a list of the diagnostics issued by the system:

1) If the password is less than 6 characters and not complex.

   "Please use a longer password."

2) If password is wrong when retyped.

   "Mismatch - password unchanged."

3) If Old password is not entered correctly.

   "Sorry."

In each case we will have to start over with the exception of diagnostic 1. In this case we must supply a longer password. We cannot change the password of another user unless we are the superuser (more on this later).

Also remember your password, because if you forget it, you cannot get into the system. When this happens you will have to go to the system administrator and have it deleted. You can then login and reset it. Some administrators assign you a temporary password "dummy" until you reset it. This is just to let you know that it shouldn't happen again.

Using the password is automatic once it has been set. Each time you login, the system will ask you for your password. You in turn must provide it or the system will not let you login.

Example:

```
UNIX   ->    login:
user   ->    dick<r>
UNIX   ->    passwd:
user   ->                        enter password, but it is not
                                 echo'd
UNIX   ->    $                   you are now in UNIX and
                                 ready to go
```

If you enter an incorrect password, the system will ask you to login again.

2.2. UNIX Command Format

Now that we are in the system we must know how to use it. We have at our disposal commands that perform various functions. These functions will be explained in detail in the later chapters. However we must know the format for them and a little about what they do. A UNIX command is simply a single word (the command itself) starting in column one and followed by a return "<r>" or a set of one or more arguments telling the command more about what it is to do. For example the "login and passwd" were both UNIX commands.

As we saw, the simplest command is a name followed by the return key. If arguments are required they follow the command separated by one or more blanks (i.e., command arg1 arg2 . . .). Lets now define the meaning for the syntax of a command (more on arguments later). For now we will just assume that they specify additional information.

1) command   The actual command (starting in column 1)
2) [ ]   Anything inside the brackets may or may not exist.
3) . . .   The preceding argument can be repeated

Lets now look at some examples and what they mean:

command [arg1 arg2]   Means that arg1 and arg2 may or may not be used with this command.

command arg . . .   Means that arg may be repeated one or more times.

command [arg . . .]   Means that arg may be repeated zero or more times.

command arg1 [arg2 . . .] [arg3]   Means that arg1 must exist, arg2 may be repeated zero or more times, and arg3 may or may not exist.

This is a very simple format and all of the UNIX commands will be defined using it. Again the meanings of the arguments will be defined later.

Next let's look at what happens when we make a mistake while entering a command. The UNIX system allows you to use the character "#" on your terminal as a means in which to cancel the previous character just entered.

Example:

| user | -> | pase#swo#d\<r\> | interpreted as "passwd" |
| user | -> | pese###asswd\<r\> | interpreted as "passwd" |

Sometimes we find that we have made too many mistakes and want to start over again. We can do this by entering the character "@". This character eliminates everything entered on that line prior to the special character "@".

Example:

| user | -> | pisewor@ | deletes everything "pisewor" |
| UNIX | -> | | no response, goes to new line |

Thus we can override some characters or if the command is too messed up, we can start over.

2.3. Exit UNIX

At some point you will be ready to quit using the UNIX system. You can just leave, or you may want to logout (exit) UNIX (i.e., bring UNIX back to the "login:" state).

There are several reasons why you should do this. The first is that the system accounting may be recording your time on the system which could result in a charge or questions of why you were on so long, and the second reason is that someone else may want to use the terminal. To exit the system you need only depress the control(cntl) key and the letter "d" at the same time. It is best to hold down the cntl key and then depress the letter d. This will result in the system responding with the login command "login:".

Example:

user –>   cntl key + letter d
UNIX –>   `login:`

If the system does not respond "login:" then try again. Make sure that you had not started a command before exiting UNIX or it may not accept the exit command.

2.4. Summary

We have now learned how to enter the UNIX system, set and use our password, a little about the UNIX command structure, correcting or eliminating typing errors, and exiting the system.

We should now try logging into and out of the system and using a password several times to assure ourselves that we understand it completely.

Once in the system you will find that the error messages provided are somewhat cryptic. In other words they do not tell you in detail what you did wrong. The most common error message provided by the system is a "?" which simply says that you did something wrong. More on error messages in the following chapters.

2.5. Questions

(1) If you do not have a login name on an available system and want one, how do you go about getting it?

(2) How do you select a login name?

(3) How long (in characters) must a password be?

(4) What do you do if you forget your password?

(5)   What character or characters are used to separate the command and its arguments?

(6)   After entering a command, what must you do to invoke the command?

(7)   How does UNIX tell you that the command issued was correct?

(8)   What is the character used by the UNIX system as a prompt?

(9)   If you enter an incorrect character what can you do to replace it with the correct character?

(10) If you entered a command and it is not correct, what can you do to correct it or replace it?

3. Creating and Maintaining Files

3.1. Creating New Text Files

Next to the UNIX system itself, the "ed" editor is one of the most important tools. Without it, it would be difficult to create and maintain text files. The "ed" editor is a line oriented editor. That is, it only allows the user to manipulate one or more lines of text or text within a line. A line is the text entered until a "return key <r>" is struck. Text can be entered in any format desired exactly the same as one would do using any typewriter.

The "ed" editor has been designed to be used on any ASCII terminal.

3.1.1. Invoking ed Editor

The first step is to start the editor and then position it such that it is ready to receive new text or modify existing text.

The format is to enter the command "ed" followed by one or more blanks and then the name of your text file. This name can consist of any legal name. A filename is limited to 14 characters. Most of the characters available on your keyboard are usable, however it is in your best interest to use combinations that are meaningful and in some way indicate what you are doing. For example, the author has named this chapter of the book "chapt3_ed". As you can see it will be very easy to locate this chapter simply by referencing its name. We know that it is chapter 3 and references the ed editor.

Once the command and text file name have been provided simply depress the return key. This will invoke the "ed" editor and will respond by 1) typing a "?" followed by the name on the next line. This question mark indicates that you have created a new text file which did not previously exist and contains no information. If a numeric (value) is returned by the system, it indicates that this text file already exists and the value represents the number of characters of text in this file.

Example:

Opening a new file

```
user   ->   ed letter<r>
ED     ->   ?letter
```

At this point you have created an empty file (i.e., no text). Always remember to depress the return key (sometimes called the carriage return key). In all the examples we will indicate the need to depress the return key by the symbol "<r>". This is very important because nothing will happen until you do depress it.

Opening an existing file.

```
user   ->   ed testdoc<r>
```

ED   ->   1234

You have now requested an existing text file named "testdoc" containing 1234 characters of text. Remember that the name originally given the file must be used to recall it. You cannot enter any name other than the name the file had been originally created with as in this case with the name "testdoc". You will learn that the computer will only interpret input that is exactly like that originally entered by you. Remember that commands must always start in column one.

Now let's assume that we have created an empty file called "letter". The first thing we will want to do is enter some text. To do this we must enter the append mode.

3.1.2. Append Mode

To enter the append mode we simply enter the command "a<r>". The system will return to a new line. No other indications will be given that you are in the append mode. At this point you can start entering any text just as if you were using a standard typewriter.

Example:

```
user     ->    a<r>
ED       ->                        no response, only positions at
                                   next line
user     ->    This is a test to see if I am<r>
user     ->    entering text in the file ''letter''.<r>
user     ->    Once I have completed it I shall find<r>
user     ->    that I have created 4 new lines of data<r>.
```

At this point let's exit the append mode. There is only one command that can be given. All other text will be entered as ordinary text to your file.

The "exit append mode" is simply a ".<r>" (period followed by a carriage return). Remember that you must have previously struck the return key "<r>" before typing the exit command if any text was entered (i.e., must be first character on a line).

Example:

```
user   ->    that I have created 4 new lines of data.<r>
user   ->    .<r>                    This will exit the append
                                     mode
```

If you had not struck the return key at the end of the last line of text and instead struck the ".<r>", it would have resulted in the "." being entered as text and the <r>would have positioned you to a new line. However, you would still be in the append mode and any new text entered would be accepted into your file.

3.1.3. Printing Text

Now that you have entered text into the file "letter", you may want to see what you have entered. First you must position yourself to the first line of text. This can be accomplished by entering the command "1p<r>". This command will position you at the first line of your text and print it. Then to print additional lines you need only depress the return key "<r>".

Example:

Let's now print the 4 lines of text entered in the file "letter"

```
user   ->    1p<r>
ED     ->    This is a test to see if I am
user   ->    <r>
ED     ->    entering text in the file ''letter''
user   ->    <r>
ED     ->    Once I have completed it I shall find
user   ->    <r>
ED     ->    that I have created 4 new lines of data.
```

You may continue this until the end of your text. The editor will respond with a "?" when the end of your text has been reached.

3.1.4. Saving Text

After entering the lines of text and viewing them you may want to exit the editor. However before you do so, you must save your work. At this point your text resides in a temporary area maintained by the editor. To save your text simply enter the command "w<r>". This will save your text in the previously named file "letter" and then respond with the number of characters in your file.

Example:

```
user    ->    w<r>
ED      ->    144
```

If the editor does not respond with the character count, be sure that you are not still in the append mode, because your file was not saved. You should get used to writing your text out to a file every now and then. There are many reasons for wanting to do this, some of which are accidental changes that destroy large parts of your file, forgetting to save your text when finishing, etc.

3.1.5. Exiting the Editor

After being sure that you have saved your text you may want to exit the editor. This is accomplished by entering the command "q<r>". This command causes you to exit the ed editor and places you under the control of the UNIX system. It is very important to remember where you are (i.e. under control of the editor or UNIX). This is because the command structure used is different for UNIX and the editor even though they appear to be very similar.

Example:(quit or exit the editor)

```
user   ->   q<r>
UNIX   ->   $                    back under UNIX control
```

3.1.6. Summary

We have now learned to create a new file, enter text, print it, save it, and exit the editor. The key points are to make sure that:

1) When creating a new file, the editor responds with a "?". Otherwise you are using an existing file.

2) When exiting the append mode you are positioned at a new line.

3) When saving your text, the editor indicates it has been saved by returning the number of characters in your file.

4) When quitting the editor the UNIX prompt appears as "$", otherwise you are still in the editor.

3.2. Maintaining Existing Files

Now that we have learned to create a new file, we can add to, delete from, and modify the text in this file. Again we request the file in the same manner that we did in creating it. However, this time we will expect the system to respond with a character count instead of "?file name"

Example:

```
user   ->   ed letter<r>
ED     ->   144
```

At this point you are now positioned at the last line of the file.

Adding to the End of Existing File

One of the requirements you will have is to add new text to the end of your existing file. To accomplish this you need only enter the command "$p<r>" which causes you to be positioned at the end of your existing text. Then you can enter the append mode command as in (section 3.2.2). Once completed, you follow the same procedures (quit append mode, save text, etc.) as defined in the previous section.

Example:

Adding new text at the end of the existing file "letter"

user	->	$p<r>	position to end of existing text
ED	->	that I have created 4 new lines of data	
user	->	a<r>	enter append mode
user	->	I will now enter two new lines of<r>	
user	->	text to see if it is accepted.<r>	
user	->	.<r>	exit append mode

At this point the file will contain the previous text plus any new text entered. It's probably a good idea to save your text using the command "w<r>". You can review it by the same procedure defined in section (3.2.4). When you first enter an existing file, you are automatically positioned at the last line. However it's a good habit to position yourself just before you perform a task.

You should also be aware that when appending anywhere other than the end of your file, new data will be inserted just after the point at which you were positioned when you entered the append mode.

Example:

Printing old and new text

user	->	1p<r>
ED	->	This is a test to see if I am
user	->	<r>

```
ED    ->    next line
```
This procedure is repeated until a "?" appears indicating the end of the file

Our text will now look as follows:

```
This is a test to see if I am
entering text in the file "letter".
Once I have completed it I shall find
that I have created 4 new lines of data.
I will now enter two new lines of
text to see if it is accepted.
```

3.2.1. Locating Text in a File

While the file contains only a few lines of text, it is not difficult to find any given line by simply printing each line as previously described. However, as the size of the file increases this may present problems. We have already learned how to position ourselves at the beginning and end of a file.

Example:

Position at beginning of a file (first line)

```
user   ->   1p<r>
ED     ->   This is a test to see if I am
       ->   Position to end of a file (last line)
user   ->   $p<r>
ED     ->   text to see if it is accepted.
```

Although this gets us to the first and last line of our file, it does not help if we need to locate text somewhere else in the file. One way is to skip over lines of text until we find what we are looking for, but first we need to know how to position ourselves. We have learned that "1p<r>" indicates the first line and "$p<r>" indicates the end of the text. We can now begin to use the command ".p<r>" to print the current line we are positioned at.

Example:

```
user   ->   1p<r>
ED     ->   This is a test to see if I am
```

At this point if we depress the return key "<r>" it causes the next line to be printed. However if we want to print the same line we can use the command ".p<r>".

Example:

```
user   ->   1p<r>
ED     ->   This is a test to see if I am
user   ->   .p<r>
ED     ->   This is a test to see if I am
```

This command is important because you can extend it to skip over lines. For example if you want to skip forward in your file "letter" two lines at a time, you simply modify your command ".p" by saying ".+2p". This states that you want to position at the current line plus 2 and print it.

Example:

```
user   ->   1p<r>                    position to first line
ED     ->   This is a test to see if I am
user   ->   .+2p<r>
ED     ->   Once I have completed it I shall find
```

You can then repeat this command which will print every other line. You can then substitute any value in place of the 2 if you would like to skip more lines at a time. For example to skip 10 lines at a time you would enter the command ".+10p<r>". You can then repeat this command as many times as you like. Once it reaches the end of the text the editor will respond with a "?" indicating that it has reached the end.

Just as we skipped forward, we can skip backward by replacing the plus sign "+" by the minus sign "-".

Example:

Position at the end of the file and skip backwards 2 lines at a time.

user	->	$p<r>	position at end of line
ED	->	text to see if it is accepted.	
user	->	.-2p<r>	position to last line minus two.
ED	->	that I have created 4 new lines of data.	

This process can be repeated to continue skipping backward until the first line in the file is located or passed. When this occurs the editor will respond with a "?".

Later we will learn other ways of locating lines of text, but for now this will be suficient for dealing with small files.

3.2.2. Inserting Text

There will be times when we have forgotten lines of text which must be included. This can be accomplished by first positioning to the line just past where you want to insert. Then by entering the command "i<r>" the editor will place you in the insert mode. You can then proceed to enter new lines of text. Each new line will be placed one after the other. Insertion will start at the line prior to where you are positioned when entering insert mode.

Example:

Insert two new lines just after the second line of existing text.

user	->	3p<r>	position after second line of text.
ED	->	Once I have completed it I shall find	
user	->	i<r>	enter insert mode
user	->	I am now inserting two lines of<r>	
user	->	text to demonstrate how it works.<r>	
user	->	.<r>	exit insert mode

Notice that the command to exit the insert mode is the same as the one for exiting the append mode. Our text will now look as follows:

> This is a test to see if I am
> entering text in the file "letter".
> I am now inserting two lines of
> text to demonstrate how it works.
> Once I have completed it I shall find
> that I have created 4 new lines of data.
> I will now enter two new lines of
> text to see if it is accepted.

3.2.3. Deleting Text

There will be many times when you find that text being entered is not what you had intended or just that you have changed your mind. When this happens you will need a way of deleting that text. This can be accomplished by positioning yourself at the line to be deleted. Then by entering the command "d<r>" you can delete the line. Notice that in the append and insert mode you position just after or at the position whereas to delete you position yourself at the line to be deleted.

Example:

Delete the two lines just previously inserted.

```
user    ->    3p<r>                    position at first line to be
                                       deleted
ED      ->    I am now inserting two lines of
user    ->    d<r>                     deletes line just printed
user    ->    d<r>                     deletes next line
```

Now that we have deleted the two lines we can look at the results. Our text will now look as follows:

> This is a test to see if I am
> entering text in the file "letter".
> Once I have completed it I shall find
> that I have created 4 new lines of data.
> I will now enter two new lines of
> text to see if it is accepted.

3.2.4. Replacing Text

To replace a line we can use the two commands "delete and insert"; however, this same task can be accomplished using a single command "change line". We first position to the line to be replaced (just as we would for delete). We then enter the command "c<r>" and proceed to enter the new line.

Example:

```
user    ->    3p<r>                    position to line being re-
                                       placed
ED      ->    Once I have completed it I shall find
user    ->    c<r>                     enter change (replace) mode
user    ->    After completion, I shall find <r>
user    ->    .<r>                     exit change mode
```

The change (replace) mode is exited the same way as append and insert modes. The example shows only one line being added. As many lines may be added as necessary or until the exit change mode ".<r>" is given. The file will now appear as:

> This is a test to see if I am
> entering text in the file "letter".
> After completion, I shall find
> that I have created 4 new lines of data.
> I will now enter two new lines of
> text to see if it is accepted.

3.2.5. Changing Contents of Line

This command allows a line to be partially changed rather than completely re-enter it. You must position to the line to be changed as with the replace or delete commands. Then you must provide the command (substitute) followed by the text to be replaced and the text that is to replace it, each separated by the seperator "/".

Format: s/old text/new text/

Example:

Restore line previously replaced to its original status.

```
user   ->   3p<r>                position to line 3
ED     ->   After completion, I shall find
user   ->   s/After completion,/Once I have
       ->   completed it/<r>
```

At this point the line has been restored to its original state. To see the resultes you may print the line by entering the command ".p<r>" or you may add a letter "p" to the end of the substitute command "s/After completion,/Once I have completed it/p".

The file will now look as follows:

```
This is a test to see if I am
entering text in the file "letter".
Once I have completed it I shall find
that I have created 4 new lines of data.
I will now enter two new lines of
text to see if it is accepted.
```

If you have to add text to the beginning or end of any single line two special indicators are provided ("^" for beginning and "$" for end). Notice that the $which was previously used to determine the end of a file is now used to determine the end of a line. The editor knows which way to use it because of the context in which it is used.

Example:

Add the text "then" to the start of line three:

```
user   ->   3p<r>                position to line 3
ED     ->   Once I have completed it I shall find
user   ->   s/^/Then /p<r>
ED     ->   Then Once I have completed it I shall find
```

Notice that we left the word "Once" capitalized. We can correct this by:

```
user   ->   s/O/o/p<r>          substitute "o" for "O"
ED     ->   Then once I have completed it I shall find
```

This same format can also be used to enter text at the end of a line.

add "to my amazement" to the end of line three.

```
user   ->   s/$/ to my amazement./p<r>
ED     ->   Then once I have completed it
       ->   I shall find to my amazement.
```

This allows you to add, delete, change anything within a single line. To delete, do not provide a replacement argument. Be very careful when using these substitutions. They must have the blanks exactly where they are needed or the text will run together. If you are trying to do the examples in this book and find that the count is different by one or two characters, it's probably because you had more or less blanks or invisible characters in your text than the examples do. Later on you will learn how to display these invisible characters.

Example:

To delete the word "Then" from the third line.

```
user   ->   s/Then //p<r>
ED     ->   once I have completed it
       ->   I shall find to my amazement.
user   ->   s/to my amazement. //p<r>
ED     ->   once I have completed it I shall find
```

We have restored the line back to its original state with the exception that the "O" on "once" must be capitalized. This could have been done at the same time we eliminated "Then", or could be done at the end by a simple substitute command "s/o/O/p<r>".

To substitute it at the same time as eliminating "Then", we would enter the command "s/Then o/O/p<r>". The string must be exactly the same as found in the file (i.e., if 2 blanks appear between "then and once" the substitute must show two blanks). One other point must be clarified before going on. The use of special characters must be treated in a special way. They are the characters "(ˆ . $[* \&)."

To make use of these characters we must place the backslash "\" in front of the special character being used. In the case of the backslash character itself, we use a double "\\" backslash to indicate a single one. Remember this is done only when you want to treat the special character as part of your text. Otherwise it has a special meaning to the ed editor (i.e., ∧ and $ as explained earlier).

3.3.6. Using Line Numbers

To this point we have dealt primarily with single line commands. We have however shown several examples that deal with line numbers. As you remember, the commands 1p, 3p, $p (line 1, line 3, last line) all dealt with specific lines. Now we will explain in greater detail the use of line numbers. We must specify a range (line n to line m) where n is the starting line number and m is the ending line number. Thus for a complete file we need only state "1,$" which indicates starting at the first line and ending at the last line. Then to create a listing of the entire program we need only state "1,$p<r>" which will cause all lines of the file to be printed out.

```
user    ->   1,$p<r>              it is assumed that the file has
                                  been opened
ED      ->   This is a test to see if I am
        ->   entering text in the file ''letter''.
        ->   Once I have completed it I shall find
        ->   that I have created 4 new lines of data.
        ->   I will now enter two new lines of
        ->   text to see if it is accepted.
```

Thus, if we know the line numbers we can create a listing of only that part of our file we require.

Example:

```
user    ->   4p<r>                positioned at the 4th line
```

We can tell what line number we are positioned at any time we choise. This can be accomplished by using the command ".=p". The editor will respond with the current line number.

Example:

user	->	.=p<r>	print line number
ED	->	4	line number at which currently positioned

This can be helpful after making numerous changes to the file. We can view several lines by providing the range "from,to". We can also use the current line indicator "." in place of the from/to number.

Example:

user	->	.,$p	print from current location to end of file
ED	->	I will now enter two new lines of	
	->	text to see if it is accepted.	

Now that we can use line numbers, let's explore how they can be used with several of the commands we have already been introduced to.

3.3.7. Printing

We have shown how one can print the entire program by first positioning to the start using "1p<r>" and then printing each line by striking the return key <r>. Now we can print any part of our file or the complete file by simply adding the "from, to" range.

Example:

user	->	1,$p<r>	print entire file
user	->	.,$p<r>	print current location to the last line in file

```
user    ->    5,10p<r>              print only lines 5 through 10
```

Remember that anytime you give a range that's beyond the text available in your file, the editor will respond with a "?". In fact, whenever there is a command sequence it does not understand it will respond with a "?". It will then be up to you to figure out what is wrong.

We can actually include the plus (+) and minus (-) in the line number expression from/to.

Example:

```
user    ->    .+5p<r>              print the 5th line past the
                                   current position
user    ->    .-5p<r>              print the 5th line preceding
                                   the current position
user    ->    $-5,$p               print the last 5 lines of the
                                   file
user    ->    .,$-10p              print from current position to
                                   10th line from end
```

As can be seen from this example we can print any combination of lines we desire. This same capability is also available on all of the following commands in this section.

3.3.8. Deleting

As with the print command we can delete any combination of lines using the same syntax, but instead of the "p" you replace it with a "d".

Example:

```
user    ->    1,$d<r>              would delete entire file
user    ->    .,$d<r>              would delete from the current
                                   location to the end of the file
```

user	->	5,10d<r>	delete lines 5 through 10
user	->	.+5d<r>	delete the 5th line after current
user	->	.-5d<r>	delete the 5th line preceding the current line
user	->	$-5,$d	delete the last 5 lines of the file
user	->	.,$-10d	delete from current position to 10th from end

It is very easy to delete lines; however, one must be careful that lines are not accidentally deleted. We described the write command (w) earlier. This command can be issued at any time during the creation and maintenance of the file.

This should be done from time to time for a number of reasons. One reason is to save work prior to complex changes. For example, if you are going to delete various lines of text, then a simple write command will assure you that all changes made prior to this can be saved. Remember that while you are adding text, deleting text, etc., you are always writing in a temporary file and not until you issue a write command will it be made permanent.

3.3.9. Searching

Now we will discuss how to locate strings of text in a file other than by skipping through the file using the line control described in section (3.3.6). With the line control range "from/to" we can now define how one can locate any string of characters in a file. It is similar in syntax to the substitute command except that there exists only one argument enclosed in "/". The format is "/text/<r>". This will cause the editor to search for the exact text pattern in the file. The editor will then stop at that line where the text pattern was found and print it.

Example:

Locate the text "I have completed it"

| user | -> | /I have completed it/<r> |

ED   `->`   `Once I have completed it I shall find`

One can search for subsequent occurrences by simply entering the characters "//" and striking the return key.

Once something else is performed (i.e., substitute, delete, etc.) the complete pattern must be reentered.

Example:

Locate all occurrences of "I have"

user   `->`   `/I have/<r>`   initiate search
ED   `->`   `Once I have completed it I shall find`
user   `->`   `//<r>`

If the "//`<r>`" is repeated it will eventually return to the first occurrence. This is because once it reaches the end of the file, it starts over again from the beginning of the file. So in the previous example if the return key is struck one more time, the results would be:

user   `->`   `//<r>`
ED   `->`   `Once I have completed it I shall find`

If there had been another occurrence of this text, the editor would have located and printed it. Since no other occurrence existed, the editor found the same occurrance as before. We have now learned a new way to locate text strings in our files. Next we will see how we can replace a text string for multiple occurrences by using a single command.

3.3.10. Substitute

Earlier we described the use of the substitute command on a single line. Now let's explore the use of it across several lines or more. The only difference between the single line use and multiple use is that we provide a range "from, to" in front of the substitute command, and a "g" (for global) at the end. Thus the syntax from our previous example would be:

```
user   ->   1,$s/after completion/Once I have
       ->   completed it/g<r>
ED     ->                        There is no response from the
                                 editor
```

The editor will locate all occurrences of "after completion" and replace it with "Once I have completed it.", but there will be no indication that it was completed.

Notice that the range "1,$" can take on any of the characteristics shown in the previous examples of print, delete, change. It is important to remember the "g", because without it the editor will only look for all occurrences on the line where you are currently positioned. It is important to note that the "g" can appear at the beginning or at the end of your command. If it appears at the beginning, it will make all the changes on that line where you are currently positioned. If, on the other hand, it appears at the end of the command, it will make all the changes within the range of lines you specify. As with the search command, the text string to be matched must be identical with the exception of some special symbols which will be defined later. If capital letters are used, or blanks, they must be included. The global substitute just described changes all occurrences in the range specified without user intervention. However, there may be occasion when you want to change only selected occurrences. This can be accomplished in one of three ways. The first is to use the search command to locate an occurrence of the string and then use the single line substitute command. However this will require entering both commands for as many occurrences as exist. We could also use the global substitute (if the number of occurrences we do not want changed are few). However in either case, it requires more effort than should be necessary. In place of these other two solutions, we can use a special conditional substitution which works the same as the global substitute just shown except that it stops at each occurrence and waits for a response from you. You can then indicate that it is to be changed or left the same. As soon as you have made your decision, the editor moves to the next one and again waits.

Example:

Change all occurrences of "I" to "you" in the file "letter"

user	->	1,$x/I/you/gp<r>	x stands for conditional command.
ED	->	this is a test to see if you am	
	->	entering text in the file ''letter''.	
	->	Once you have completed it you shall find	
	->	that you have created 4 new lines of data.	
	->	You will now enter two new lines of	
	->	text to see if it is accepted.	

When the editor stops at an "I", you must depress the "." key to accept.
The Return key will skip to the next match.
Change all occurrences of "you" back to "I"

user	->	1,$x/you/I/gp<r>
user	->	1,$p<r>
ED	->	This is a test to see if I am
	->	entering text in the file ''letter''.
	->	Once I have completed it I shall find
	->	that I have created 4 new lines of data.
	->	I will now enter two new lines of
	->	text to see if it is accepted.

Both global substitute commands "s" and "x" are very useful when a string must be changed throughout a large text file.

3.2.11. Change Command

As with the other commands, the change command may contain a range (from, to). This range will cause those lines to be deleted, and the editor will then wait for new text to be entered. Once a ".<r>" is encountered by the editor it exits the change mode and awaits a new command.

Example:

Remove 4 lines of text and replace it with 2 lines of text. The file looked as follows prior to the change command:

> This is a test to see if you am
> entering text in the file "letter".
> Once you have completed it you shall find
> that you have created 4 new lines of data.
> you will now enter two new lines of
> text to see if it is accepted.

```
user   ->   3,6c<r>
user   ->   This is line 1 replacement <r>
user   ->   This is line 2 replacement <r>
user   ->   .<r>
user   >    1,$p<r>
ED     ->   This is a test to see if you am
       ->   entering text in the file ''letter''.
       ->   This is line 1 replacement
       ->   This is line 2 replacement
```

This command is useful when several lines must be replaced rather than just changed.

3.2.12. Moving Text

Quite frequently you will find it necessary to move one or more lines to another location in the text. This can be accomplished by use of the move command (m). You must specify the range (from,to) lines to be moved, followed by the move command (m) and it in turn followed by the line number where the text is to be moved to (i.e., "from,to m where").

The from,to range represents the lines to be moved. The "where" line indicates that the text will be moved, starting after that line.

Example:

Move lines 1 and 2 to the end of the file (letter)

Prior to the change command, the file "letter" looks as follows:

    This is a test to see if I am
    entering text in the file "letter".
    Once I have completed it I shall find
    that I have created 4 new lines of data.
    I will now enter two new lines of
    text to see if it is accepted.

user   ->   1,2 m $<r>

The file "letter" looks as follows after the move:

user   ->   1,$p<r>
ED   ->   Once I have completed it I shall find
            ->   that I have created 4 new lines of data.
            ->   I will now enter two new lines of
            ->   text to see if it is accepted.
            ->   This is a test to see if I am
            ->   entering text in the file ``letter''.

As we can see by this example, we can move any amount of text to another place in the file by use of this command. This is generally known as cut and paste, because we are taking (cutting) text from one part of the file and puting (pasting) it in another part of the file.

3.2.13. Write File, Read File

There will be times when text from a particular file will be used in other files and possibly within the same file. The write command allows you to save the entire file or any part of that file in another file. You can use the read command to read any existing file into the file you are currently editing.

The command to write out the current file you are editing is "w". We have already used this command when saving our file. However when using the "w" by itself we are saving our text into the file having the same name as we used in invoking the file. To write the current file being edited to another file having a different name, we simply enter the write command followed by one or more spaces and the name of our new file.

Example:

Let's assume we are currently editing the file "letter" and we are about to make some major changes. If we think that it is wise or necessary to save the text as it currently exists we can simply enter the following command:

user	->	w temp<r>
ED	->	272

The number of characters written

The new file "temp" now contains the same text as does "letter". However once the file "temp" has been written out, any changes to "letter" will not be reflected in "temp".

Example:

Another case is where you want to save only part of the current file being edited. This is done using the same command as before, except that you specify the from/to range as used on other commands(i.e., p,d,s,etc.).

Using the same example as before, but writing out only the first 3 lines we would say:

user	->	1,3w temp<r>

Remember that in both examples, if anything existed in the file "temp" it will be replaced by the the write "w" command upon execution. The new file "temp" will look as follows:

> This is a test to see if I am
> entering text in the file "letter".
> Once I have completed it I shall find

Now let's look at how we can read these files and place the text from them into the current file being edited. We have two formats for reading text into the file being edited. The first is just an "r file" which will read the complete file and append it to the end of the file being edited. The second format is to position yourself to the line in your current file and issue ".r file". This command will read the complete file and append it just after the current position(specified by ".").

Example:

Let's read the 3 lines of text just saved in the file temp and place it at the end of the file letter. The current file "letter" looks as:

> This is a test to see if I am
> entering text in the file "letter".
> Once I have completed it I shall find
> that I have created 4 new lines of data.
> I will now enter two new lines of
> text to see if it is accepted.

```
user   ->    r temp<r>
ED     ->    99
```
                                                   number of characters just read

The file now looks like:

```
user   ->    1,$p<r>
ED     ->    This is a test to see if I am
```

```
->    entering text in the file ''letter''.
->    Once I have completed it I shall find
->    that I have created 4 new lines of data.
->    I will now enter two new lines of
->    text to see if it is accepted.
->    This is a test to see if I am
->    entering text in the file ''letter''.
->    Once I have completed it I shall find
```

Again remember that until we write the current file out, what we see here is only in a temporary buffer. Now to read the same lines in, but just after line 3, we will say:

```
user   ->   3p<r>                  position to line 3
ED     ->   Once I have completed it I shall find
user   ->   .r temp<r>
ED     ->   99                     number of characters just
                                   read in
user   ->   1,$p<r>
ED     ->   This is a test to see if I am
       ->   entering text in the file ''letter''.
       ->   Once I have completed it I shall find
       ->   This is a test to see if I am
       ->   entering text in the file ''letter''.
       ->   Once I have completed it I shall find
       ->   that I have created 4 new lines of data.
       ->   I will now enter two new lines of
       ->   text to see if it is accepted.
```

The write and read commands can be very powerful when you need to save parts of an existing file and later use them in a new file.

3.2.14. The Undo Command "u"

There will be times when you find that a change you just made was not necessary or wrong. The Undo command "u" can be used to restore the line just changed to its previous state by typing the command "u<r>".

Example: (restore a changed line to its original state)

We have a line of text as follows:

I will now enter two new lines of

And we change it as follows:

I wil not want to new lines of

Now to change it back without having to retype it we say:

```
user   ->   u<r>
ED     ->   I will now enter two new lines of
```

This command can only be used immediately after making the changes. If you go elsewhere within the file and do something else you will find that entering the command "u" will have no effect on the previous change. In fact, it will change the current line that may have just been edited.

3.3. Special Uses

There are many special ways in which the editor can be used. As you use it try different things and see how they work. In this section we will provide you with a few ideas of things that can be done.

3.3.1. The List Command "l"

The editor provides two commands for printing the contents of the lines you are editing. We have already described one of them which is "p". The second command "l", meaning list, provides more information than can be obtained by using the "p" command. Its main attribute is that it makes characters that are normally invisible, visible, such as tabs and backspaces. In addition to this, the "l" command will fold long lines for printing. For example any line that exceeds 72 characters is printed on multiple lines. To tell that it was folded and where it was folded, a backslash "\" is inserted at the end of each part of a line folded.

Some of the invisible characters are:

o tab   – printed as >
o backspace   – printed as <
o form feed   – printed as 014
o vertical tab   – printed as 013
o bell   – printed as \07
o new line   – printed as \n

Generally when these special characters appear, it is because you have accidently typed one of these characters.

Example:


```
user   ->   1,$l<r>
ED     ->   This is a test to see if I am>
       ->   enterin\07g text in the file ''letter''.
       ->   Once I have completed it I shall find
       ->   This is a test to see if I am
       ->   entering text in the file ''letter''.
```


We have two invisible characters in this file. The first is a tab ">" and the second is the bell character "\07". We would have never known they were there if not for the "l" command.

3.3.2. Use of Metacharacters

You were previously introduced to certain characters that have special meanings when they occur on the left side of a substitute command, or in a search for a particular line. These special characters are often called metacharacters.

The Metacharacter "."

This character when used on the left side of a substitute command, or in a search, stands for any single character.

Example: (represent any single character)

Find an occurrence in the file "letter" that contains "e" and "t" separated by any single character.

```
user   ->   /e.t/<r>
ED     ->   This is a test to see if I am
user   ->   //.<r>
ED     ->   entering text in the file ''letter''.
```

We can see by this example that the first occurrence is the word "test" with the "e.t" being the "est". The next occurrence is on the next line and is the word "entering" with the "e.t" being the "ent".

This command is useful when dealing with invisible characters as we defined in section 3.4.1. If, for example, we have text which contains one of these invisible characters, we can get rid of it by substituting as follows:

Example:

We have a line which contains the bell character "\07".

the line of text is:

enterin\07g text in the file "letter".

```
user   ->   s/enterin.g/entering/p<r>
ED     ->   entering text in the file ''letter''.
```

Notice that the bell character appears as three characters "\07". However it is actually only represented as a single character internally and the "." will work.

You must make sure that the "." metacharacter is used properly. Since it matches any character, you must be sure that the pattern is exact or the results may not be what you intended.

3.3.2.1. The Metacharacter "*"

The metacharacter "*", or star, is used to indicate that a character followed by the "*" is to stand for any characters following.

Example:

If we have a large number of spaces between some text, we can suppress the spaces to a single space by saying:

The text is: "The file   as we know it."

```
user    ->    s/e *as/e as/p<r>
ED      ->    The file as we know it.
```

3.3.2.2. The Metacharacters "[ ]"

The metacharacters "[ ]" allow you to specify a number of characters that you may want to recognize when performing an operation.

Example:

The text is:

1 The cat is yellow
2 Why do you care
3 How is it going

```
user    ->    1,$s/^[0-9]//p<r>
ED      ->    The cat is yellow
        ->    Why do you care
        ->    How is it going
```

As we can see from this example we can delete any digit that appears at the beginning of a line. The characters in the brackets are refered to as a character class which can be used in place of a series of single commands.

3.3.2.3. The Metacharacter "&"

The metacharacter "&" is used primarily to save typing.

Example:

If we have a line of text:

"This is how the Gauthier's recognize their dog."

We could change this to say:

"This is how the Gauthier's can recognize their dog."

by entering the command:

```
user    ->   s/Gauthier's/Gauthier's can/p<r>
ED      ->   This is how the Gauthier's can recognize their dog.
```

We should not have to repeat the name Gauthier's and this is where the "&" can be used to replace it.

```
user    ->   s/Gauthier's/& can/p<r>
ED      ->   This is how the Gauthier's can recognize their dog.
```

3.3.2.4   The Metacharacters " $, ˆ "

We have already talked about the metacharacters "$ and ˆ". But for a quick review we will show a couple of examples.

The "$" depending on how it is used can indicate the end of your file, or the end of a line. When used as a range (line 1 to line $) it is clear that we are talking about the end of the file "1,$p" will print the entire file. However the command "s/$/./p" will indicate that the period "." will be placed at the end of the current line.

Example:

line of text:

this is the

```
user    ->    s/$/end of line/p<r>
ED      ->    this is the end of line
```

The metacharacter "^" is the same as the "$" except that it indicates the beginning of a line instead of the end. By reversing the previous example we can see:

The line of text is:

end of line

```
user    ->    s/^/this is the/p<r>
ED      ->    this is the end of line
```

3.4. Summary

As we stated before, the editor is one of the most important and most frequently used commands. Without it you will not be able to create and maintain files.

We have not been able to show all the possible ways in which you can use this editor. The best way to learn is to try different things and see if they work. In our examples we have shown the log form of how each function works. Try taking short cuts (assume that the editor understands some of the information already) and see what happens.

3.5. Questions

(1) When you invoke a file using "ed", how can you

    a) tell if it's a new file?

    b) tell that it's an existing file?

(2) When entering the append mode, where do you start adding data?

(3) How do you exit the append mode?

(4) For each of the following commands, describe:

    - how it is invoked

    - how you exit from it (if appropriate)

    - what its function is

    - what change takes place (position)

        a) append

        b) insert

        c) change

        d) delete

        e) print

(5) What is the procedure for replacing part of a line of text?

(6) What is the procedure to save text once it has been entered?

    How do you know that it has been saved?

(7) what command is used to exit the editor?

(8) What is the command used to print the entire file?

(9) What indication is given (if any) when the end of the file is reached?

(10) What is the meaning of each of the following characters:

        a) $

        b) ^

        c) *

d) g

e) ?

(11) Describe the function performed by each of the following commands:

a) .=p

b) .-1p

c) .+1p

d) .p

e) 1,3c

new line of text

.

f) .,.+3d

g) /The/

h) s/^/The/p

i) 1,$w newfile

j) s/$/$/p

k) gs/you/I/p

l) s/I/you/pg

4. The UNIX File System

Now that we know how to log into the UNIX system and create files, we should know a little about where we are and what we can do.

The UNIX file system is a hierarchical file system and plays a very important role in the overall usage of the system. The user has access to 3 kinds of files: ordinary disk files, directories, and special files.

Ordinary files are those created by the user as we defined in chapter three. They contain whatever information the user places in them. A file of text consists simply of a string of characters. They may represent normal text such as documents, computer programs, or whatever else the user may want.

Special files constitute the most unusual feature of the UNIX file system and will be described in more detail in chapter 9.

Directories provide the mapping between the names of files and the files themselves, and thus induce a structure on the file system as a whole. The system maintains several directories for its own use. One of these is the root directory. All files in the system can be found by tracing a path through a chain of directories until the desired file is reached. The starting point for such searches is often at the root. Each user generally has a directory assigned by the systems administrator. This directory is known as the user home directory for that particular user. This home directory differs from the system root directory in that it is used by that user only. This is accomplished by the fact that the file system is hierarchical in its structure. The following example shows its format.

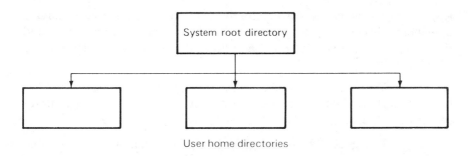

User home directories

User home directories

figure 4.1

The example above shows only one level of the file system (i.e., root, and user home directories). Each of the user home directories in turn can have subdirectories. The user who owns that particular user root may set up any number of files and subdirectories within his own home directory.

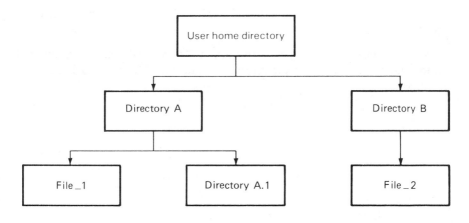

figure 4.2

The number of files and directories available to each user is only limited by system parameters for all files and directories. This is not the concern of the user but of the system administrator. If the system runs out of space, it is the duty of the administrator to see how it can be fixed, which might include requests to the users to eliminate files or directories. See chapter 9 on the duties of the system administrator.

As we can see from the file system in figure 4.2, we have a user home directory and under it two subdirectories (directory A and directory B). Then we find a file and directory under directory A and a file under directory B.

When the user logs into the system (s)he is positioned at his/her **home directory. Then from this directory (s)he can move to any subdirectories or files.**

In figure 4.2, once logged in the user has access from his/her home directory A or B. Once moved to directory A the user has access to file 1 or directory A.1. Notice that the user does not have access to file 1 directly from the home directory. (S)he must first position to directory A. Thus a user has immediate access to any file directly under a given directory, but to access files under subdirectories it is is necessary to position to that subdirectory prior to accessing the file.

This leads us to the definition of a "pathname". A pathname is a series of directory names separated by "/" and ending in either a directory name or a file name (depends on its usage).

Now let's look at all the legal pathnames that may exist in figure 4.2.

Let's say the user login name is "dick" and that his home directory is "dick". Then the pathnames available to him under his home directories are:

A

B

A/file_1

A/A.1

B/file_2

Notice that the user home directory "dick" is not included in the pathnames. This is because it becomes the base and everything else is an extension of this base. Thus in order for us to access file_1, we must position ourselves at directory A and then we have access to it. Remember that we cannot include a file name in a path unless it is the last name in the path and even this depends on how the path is used (more on this later).

The "/" character used to separate pathnames is to be used very carefully as it can be interpreted in several ways.

For example a pathname not started with a "/" causes the system to begin the search in the user's current directory. If the user is in his/her home directory then the pathname A/A.1 will start looking for the directory A in the home directory "dick" and then look for the directory A.1 in the directory A.

If you are looking for a directory or file and the pathname you gave is incorrect, the system will respond as:

```
path    ->    A/A.2
UNIX    ->    A/A.2: bad directory
        ->    $
```

The system simply prints the pathname you requested and the message "bad directory".

4.1. Knowing Where You Are

When you get a message telling you that a pathname is bad, and you know it exists, you will want to try to find it. The first UNIX command we will use once logged into the system is the command "pwd" which when issued provides you with the pathname specifying where you are.

Command:	pwd
Syntax:	pwd
Function:	Prints the pathname of the current directory.

Example: Let's say we are positioned in directory A.1

```
user   ->   pwd
UNIX   ->   /dick/A/A.1
       ->   $
```

Notice that the pwd command provides the complete pathname including the user home directory. If there was a file system directory it would also be provided. This is useful when you are not sure just where you are and need this information to get back to another directory. The file system directory is controlled by the system administrator and should not cause you any trouble. However you must know that it exists if you want to use a complete pathname to get to a particular directory. The "pwd" command will provide you with all the information necessary to allow you to use a complete pathname.

Example: let's say that the file system direc-
                                               tory name is "usr". Then to see
                                               our current directory "A.1" we
                                               will say:

```
user   ->   pwd<r>
UNIX   ->   /usr/dick/A          assuming that we are in A
       ->   $
```

In this case, as in the previous case, we see that the "/" is at the start of the pathname. This indicates that the system will start searching from the system root directory and not from your user home directory. If we were to issue the command "pwd" just after login, we would see "/usr/dick" displayed as our current pathname.

4.1.1. Contents of a Directory

Next we will want to see what files and directories we have in our current directory. To see what the names are in our current directory we can issue the command "ls". This command will give us a list of all names in alphabetical order.

Example: Currently positioned in the direc-
                               tory /usr/dick

```
user    ->    ls<r>
UNIX    ->    A
        ->    B
        ->    $
```

As we can see only the names are provided. We must remember which are directories and which are files. Again, as we stated before, only the directories and files directly under the current directory are shown. In other words files 1 and 2 and directory A.1 are not shown.

4.1.2. Changing Directories

To enable us to see the files and directories at the lower levels, we can use the command "cd pathname". This will position us at the directory whose name was the last one in the pathname(i.e., /usr/dick/A would result in the system being positioned to directory A). If we know where we are, we do not have to provide the complete pathname, only the extension from where we are to where we want to be.

Example: After login see where we are,
                               list names in home directory,
                               and change to one of the subdi-
                               rectories.

```
user   ->   pwd<r>              get current pathname
UNIX   ->   /usr/dick           current directory
       ->   $
```

```
user   ->   ls<r>               list names in current direc-
                                tory
UNIX   ->   A
       ->   B
       ->   $
user   ->   cd A<r>             change to directory A
UNIX   ->   $                   ready for next command
user   ->   pwd<r>              see where we are
UNIX   ->   /usr/dick/A         current directory
       ->   $
user   ->   ls<r>               list names in directory A
UNIX   ->   A.1
       ->   file_1
       ->   $
```

We can now see where we are in our file system, see what directories and files we have in our current(working) directory, and change to a
new directory. Let's now look at how we can change to a directory that is
not a subdirectory to the one we are currently positioned in. To be sure,
we can always provide the complete pathname to the directory we want.
However there are shorter ways to describe it. In the previous example we
positioned ourselves in the directory A. The only directory we can change
to going forward (next subdirectory) is directory A.1. However if we want
to go to directory B we will have to state the complete pathname. Let's
look at the different ways in which we can change to another directory
regardless of where it is.

Example: Changing to another directory

```
user   ->   pwd<r>
UNIX   ->   /usr/dick
       ->   $
user   ->   cd A/A.1              change to directory A.1
UNIX   ->   $                     now positioned at A.1
user   ->   cd ../               change back to A
UNIX   ->   $                     now positioned at A
user   ->   cd ../B              change to directory B
UNIX   ->   $                     now positioned at B
user   ->   cd ../A/A.1          change back to A.1
UNIX   ->   $                     now positioned at A.1
user   ->   cd ../../            change back to dick
UNIX   ->   $                     now positioned at dick
```

As you can see from the various ways of changing directories, it could be very easy to get lost. Just remember that anytime you are not sure where you are, you can issue the "pwd" command.

Also as can be seen from the examples shown, you must always provide a direct path to a given directory. In the example "cd . ./B" you see that you had to go back to the directory dick (i.e., . ./ takes you back one directory) and then forward to the directory B. This is because there was no other way to get to the directory B.

4.2. Directories and Files

Earlier we saw that the command "ls" would provide us with a list of the names of directories and files in the current directory. However it did not tell us which ones were directories and which ones were files. We can extend the command "ls" by adding an argument that will provide us with additional information. By adding the argument "-l" (the letter l) to the ls command we will be provided with the following information.

Example:

```
user   ->   ls -l<r>
```

```
UNIX  ->    total 2
      ->    drwxrwxr-x 2 dick    32 Dec 30 18:54 A
      ->    drwxrwxr-x 2 dick    32 Dec 30 18:55 B
      ->    $
```

There is much more information here then we need at this time, but let's quickly review it.

o   The d indicates that this entry is a directory
o   The rwxrwxr-x specifies permissions(more later)
o   The 2 specifies the number of links(more later)
o   The name dick specifies the owner of the entry
o   The value 32 is the size in characters
o   The next entry is the date last modified
o   The name A or B is the name of the directory

The main thing to remember for now is that the "d" indicates that the entry is a directory. If it had been a file, then the "d" would have been replaced with "-". The other is the name of the file or directory. The remaining items in the entry will be explained later.

4.2.1. Creating and Deleting Directories

To this point in the discussion, we have assumed that the directories were always there. However the only directory available for a new user is the user home directory created by the system administrator. Any other directories under this home directory must be created by the user, and when the user is finished with them (s)he must delete them, or just let them exist unused. To create a new directory a user must position to where the directory is to be created. In the case of a new user it is not necessary, because the only directory that exists is his/her home directory. Once positioned to where the directory is to be created, the user enters "mkdir directory name".

Command: mkdir

Syntax: mkdir directory . . .

Function: The command mkdir (make directory) creates one
                         or more new directories.

Option: No options exist for this command.
Example: For a new user create directories A and B


```
user    ->    mkdir A B<r>
UNIX    ->    $                    Indicates directories created
user    ->    pwd<r>
UNIX    ->    /usr/dick
user    ->    ls<r>
UNIX    ->    A
        ->    B
        ->    $
```

The new directories would appear as follows:

figure 4.3

　　　　Notice that after the directories are created you remain in your
current directory. The directories A and B have been created and to use
them you must change directories(cd) to one of them. Once changed you
may create new directories or files under them. You do not have to create
all directories at once. You may create them anytime, as you need them.

There will be times when you are permanently through with a directory. When this happens you should delete it. This is because it does take space in the system and the system storage could fill up if no one ever deleted their files and directories. To delete a directory you must be positioned in the directory that references the one to be deleted. In the previous case we created two directories A and B and were positioned in the user home directory (see figure 4.3). So to delete the directories A and B we first make sure that we are in the home directory "/usr/dick". Now we simply say "rmdir directory name".

Command: rmdir

Syntax: rmdir directory . . .

Function: The command rmdir(remove directory) does just what it says; it removes one or more directories from the system. You must be sure that when you remove a directory no files or subdirectories exist in the directory being deleted.

Option: No options exist for this command.
Example: Remove directories A and B

user	->	rmdir A B<r>	
UNIX	->	$	indicates directories have been removed
user	->	pwd<r>	
UNIX	->	/usr/dick	
	->	$	ready to accept next command
user	->	ls<r>	
UNIX	->	$	indicates nothing in root directory

Once the directories A and B have been deleted, your home directory is the only one remaining.

```
┌─────────────────────────┐
│                         │
│   User home directory   │
│                         │
└─────────────────────────┘
```

figure 4.4

As we can see from figure 4.4, the only thing that remains is the home directory for "dick". We do not ever want to delete our own home directory. If we do, we will not be able to login again. This will be better understood when you read chapter 9 on the duties of the system administrator.

4.2.2. Removing Files

We have discussed the creation and deletion of directories(mkdir, rmdir) and a way of creating files(ed editor). Now we will show one way of deleting files. Thus we will be able to create and delete both directories and files. To delete a file we must position ourselves in the directory where the file exists and then simply issue the command "rm filename".

Example:

Let's say we have created the files file1, file2 and file3 under our home directory.

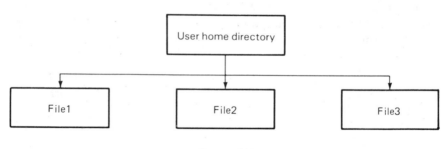

figure 4.5

```
user   ->   rm file1 file3<r>
UNIX   ->   $                    files removed
user   ->   pwd<r>
UNIX   ->   /usr/dick
       ->   $
user   ->   ls<r>
UNIX   ->   file2
       ->   $
```

We can see from these examples that the creation and deletion of both files and directories are performed in a similar way. In other words in all cases you must be positioned in the correct directory, and the only indication from UNIX that it has performed its task correctly is the prompt sign "$". If it had not performed its task, it would have issued one of the following diagnostics depending on the command issued.

- If it doesn't exist(wrong directory or name)
  "rm: filename nonexistent"
  "rmdir: directoryname nonexistent"
- If you do not own the file or directory
  "rm: filename non-existent"
  "rmdir: directoryname non-existent"

4.2.3. Permissions

At this point we have not yet talked about permissions, that is who can read and/or write on a file. This is very important, because you can get in a lot of trouble if you try to access something that you do not have permission to see. Remember earlier we showed you how to tell a directory from a file. There was some other information there that was not necessary at the time; however, now it is appropriate to know a little more about it. Let's start by reviewing the example in section 4.2. By using the "ls -l" command we can see the information we need.

Example:

```
user   ->   ls -l<r>
UNIX   ->   total 2
       ->   drwxrwxr-x 2 dick    32 Dec 30 18:54 A
       ->   drwxrwxr-x 2 dick    32 Dec 30 18:55 B
       ->   $
```

We have already explained some of the information, but let's quickly review it again.

o   The d indicates that this entry is a directory

o   The rwxrwxr-x specifies permissions

o   **The 2 specifies the no of links**

o   The name dick specifies the owner of the entry

o   The value 32 is the size in characters

o   The next entry is the date last modified

o   The name A or B is the name of the directory

What we need to understand is just what the permissions(rwxrwx..) mean. UNIX provides three(3) levels of protection to each owner of a file or directory. They include:

o   read/write/execute permission for the owner

o   read/write/execute permission for the group

o   read/write/execute permission for all others

First let's understand who the owner, group, and others are and how and where they are set.

The owner is the one who is logged in. In our previous examples "dick" was the one logged in and is the owner of all files and directories created by him. Thus when a "ls -l" command is issued the owner's login name will appear immediately after the permissions and group number:

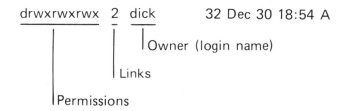

Now let's look at the specific meaning of the permissions. If we read from left to right we will see three (3) sets of "rwx's". The first group is the read/write/execute permission for the owner, the second group is the read/write/execute permission for the group, and the third is the read/write/execute permission for all others. These permissions can be set by the system and by individuals (owners, groups, etc.). How we set them will be described in more detail in chapter 5. We can now see each of the permissions and their meanings.

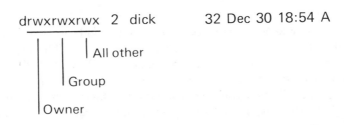

r = read permission, if "-" then no read permission

w = write permission, if "-" then no write permission

x = execute permission, if "-" then no execute permission

Example:

-rwxrwxrwx 2 dick   32 Dec 30 18:54 A

This entry means that A is a file and everyone has read/write/execute permission.

-rw-rw-r-- 2 dick   32 Dec 30 18:54 A

This entry means that A is a file and the owner and group have read/write permission and all others have only read permission.

-rw-r–r– 2 dick   32 Dec 30 18:54 A

This entry means that A is a file and only the owner (dick) has read/write permission while the group and all others have read permission only.

-rw– 2 dick   32 Dec 30 18:54 A

This entry means that A is a file and only the owner (dick) has read/write permission. The group and all others cannot access the file.

-rwxr-xr-x 2 dick   32 Dec 30 18:54 A

This entry means that A is a file and only the owner (dick) has permission to write. Everybody has permission to read and execute the file.

4.3. Summary

You should make sure that you understand the basic principles explained in this chapter before going on to the next. The file structure and how you use it is essential in the overall ease with which UNIX can help you. First make sure that you understand what a hierarchical file system is and then how you find your way through it. The next important item is to understand the meaning of a pathname and the various ways in which it can be constructed.

4.4. Questions

(1) When you first log into the system where are you positioned?

(2) How many subdirectories and files can you have at any one time?

(3) What type of file system used by UNIX?

Define it.

(4) If you are not sure where you are in the file system at any given time, what can you do to find out where you are?

(5) Define the function of each of the following commands:

a) ls

b) cd

c) mkdir

d) rmdir

e) rm

(6) How can you tell directory names from file names?

(7) What are the three levels of read/write permissions allowed under UNIX?

(8)   Using the following file structure under the user home directory
      "dick", describe the function of each of the following commands
      and what effect they will have on the file structure if executed (as-
      sume that they are executed in the order they appear).

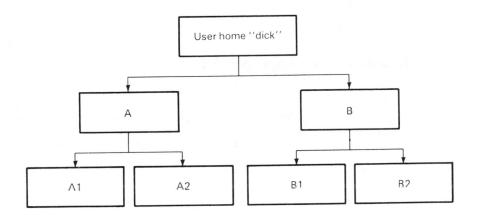

a) login dick

b) cd A/A1

c) cd ../A2

d) cd ../../B

e) rmdir B1

f) rmdir A1

g) pwd

h) mkdir B1.1

5. Manipulation of Files

Now that you have learned how to log into the system, and some manipulation of files and directories, you can extend this knowledge with the following commands. The ability to move or copy files from one place to another, list and archive files, and in general provide for the management of your files is needed. UNIX provides a wealth of commands for providing these capabilities. The following commands are directly related to this and are explained in the following sections.

5.1. Concatenation of Files

Command:	cat
Syntax:	cat [-u] [file1. . .]
Function:	The usage of this command is to concatenate one or more files and direct the results to your terminal, a file, or another command.

Option: Only one option exists for this command "-u". It
                           is used to change the block size of the output when
                           a size other then the default "512-byte blocks" are
                           required.

Example:

(1) The simplest and most frequent use of this command is for printing the
     contents of a file on your terminal. If you would like to see the contents
     of a file named "file1" you could enter "cat file1" and immediately see
     the results.


```
user   ->   cat file1 <r>
UNIX   ->   1 line one
       ->   3 line three
       ->   7 line seven
       ->   6 line six
       ->   2 line two
       ->   5 line five
       ->   4 line four
       ->   $
```

     As can be seen from these results, it is a very fast way to see the
contents of any file.

(2) A more representative way of using the cat command is to combine
     several files. This is useful when several people are working on a report
     and the results are to be output as a single copy. You have four files
     "a,b,c,d" each containing some text. To see all of them you need only
     say "cat a b c d" and the results will appear on your terminal.


```
user   ->   cat a b c d <r>
UNIX   ->   a a a a a
       ->   b b b b b
       ->   c c c c c
       ->   d d d d d
       ->   $
```

Notice that the order in which the files are given in the cat command is the order in which they are concatenated.

```
user    ->    cat d c b a <r>
UNIX    ->    d d d d d
        ->    c c c c c
        ->    b b b b b
        ->    a a a a a
        ->    $
```

(3) The results of a cat command can be directed to another file or command as well as to the terminal. To accomplish this we can enter "cat a b c d >e" which will place the results in the file named "e".

```
user    ->    cat a b c d > e <r>
UNIX    ->    $
```

The only indication that the command has completed is the UNIX prompt sign "$". However the results are now in the file "e". To view them we can enter "cat e" and the results are:

```
a a a a a
b b b b b
c c c c c
d d d d d
$
```

(4) The cat command can also be used to enter data into a new file. This is accomplished by not entering a name of an input file. We say "cat >x" and the command will wait for input from your terminal.

```
user    ->    cat >x <r>
```

```
->    This is a test to see if I can
->    enter new text into the file x.
->                    <ctrl>-d
->    $
```

The "<ctrl>-d" was necessary to terminate the input and save the data just entered in the file x.

```
user  ->   cat x <r>
UNIX  ->   This is a test to see if I can
      ->   enter new text into the file x.
      ->   $
```

Again remember that the "$" is the prompt from UNIX telling you that it is ready for another command.

Summary:

The syntax is very simple. You must have at least one blank after the command and each of the input files specified. However the output direction does not require blanks and therefore they are used only for readability. This is probably a good habit to get used to.

5.2. Copy Files

Command: cp

Syntax: cp file1 file2

                   or

                   cp file1. . . filen directory

Function: This command is used to copy one file to another or several files to a directory. The files being copied are not affected. However if the new file already existed it will be lost and the contents will be those of the file being copied.

Option: No options exist other than the specific usage described in the syntax.

Example:

(1) Simply copy one file to another. Copy file "aa" to file "aa1", where file "aa" contains:

```
1 1 2 1 1
2 2 1 2 2
```

We enter the command:

```
user   ->   cp aa aa1 <r>
UNIX  ->   $
```

The "$" indicates that the copy was completed and the new file "aa1" contains the same data as the file "aa". Remember that if the file "aa1" already existed its previous contents are lost. To see the contents of the new file we need only execute the cat command.

```
user   ->   cat aa1 <r>
UNIX  ->   1 1 2 1 1
        ->   2 2 1 2 2
        ->   $
```

(2) Now let's copy several files to a new directory. The files "a b c d" will be copied to the directory "dir1". As before, any files in the new directory with the same name will be replaced with the files being copied. To execute this function we enter:

```
user   ->   cp a b c d dir1 <r>
UNIX  ->   $
```

We can now change directories to "dir1" and perform an "ls" command to see if the files have been moved.

```
user   ->   cd dir1 <r>
       ->   ls dir1 <r>
UNIX  ->   a
       ->   b
       ->   c
       ->   d
       ->   $
```

If other files already existed in the directory "dir1" they would also be displayed.

Summary:

This command is useful when backup copies are required. You can change the original copy and if you need to recover to its previous state, you can by simply copying it back.

5.3. Move Files

Command: mv

Syntax: mv file1 file2

                  or

                  mv directory1 directory2

or

mv file1...filen directory2

Function: This command is similar to the copy command
                     with the exception being that the original file is
                     deleted. One additional feature is the ability to
                     move a complete directory to another one.

Option: No options exist other than those in the syntax.

Example:

(1) The first example will be moving one file to another. We will move
     the file "aa1" created in the copy example to a file called "aa2".

```
user   ->   mv aa1 aa2 <r>
UNIX   ->   $
```

     If we now execute the command "ls" we can see that only the file
"aa2" exists. The file "aa1" has been deleted. However, the contents of
"aa2" are exactly the same as were the contents of "aa1". If we made
a mistake, we can still recover by copying the file "aa2" back to "aa1".
Notice that if we had moved it back we would have lost "aa2".

(2) Now let's move all of the files in one directory to a second directory.
     We could do this by using the format "mv file1...filen directory2" or
     by simply specifying the two directories "mv directory1 directory2".
     In the first case we would be required to name each of the files being
     moved, whereas in the second case we need only name the directories,
     which would require that all files be moved. Let's say that directory1
     contains the files a b c and d. And the new directory "directory2"
     contains the files x and y. We now execute the command:

```
user    ->   mv directory1 directory2 <r>
```

UNIX -> $

We can now list the files in the first directory which will show no files. Then let's list the files in the second directory which will display the four files moved plus the two files already there.

user   ->   ls directory1 <r>
UNIX   -> $

The "$" response indicates no files.

user   ->   ls directory2 <r>
UNIX   ->   a
           ->   b
           ->   c
           ->   d
           ->   x
           ->   y
           -> $

Summary:

The two things to be careful about are (1) that you have deleted the file(s) being moved and (2) that any files by the same name will be replaced.

5.4. Print File

Command: pr

Syntax: pr [option]. . . [file]. . .

Function:	This command produces a printed listing of one or more files. The output is separated into pages with a heading on each page consisting of the name of the file and the date and time of the printing. The options can alter this somewhat. The output is directed to the standard output unless you redirect it(see chapter 6 on redirection).
Option:	The following options can be used with the pr command:

-n	Produce n-column output where n can be any number of columns that will fit on a page.
+n	Start the printing n pages into the file.
-h	take the next argument as the page header instead of the default header.
-wn	When multi-column output is selected, take the width of the page to be n characters instead of the default (72 characters).
-ln	Change the length of the page to be n lines instead of the default (66 lines).
-t	Do not print the 5 line header or the 5 line trailer normally supplied for each page.
-sc	Separate columns by the single character c instead of by the appropriate amount of white space. A missing c is treated as a tab.
-m	Print all files simultaneously, each in one column.

Example:

(1) Print a file with the header automatically generated.

```
user   -> pr letter
UNIX   -> Dec 20 14:54 1980 letter Page 1
       -> This is a test to see if I am
       -> entering text in the file ''letter''.
```

```
        ->    Once I have completed it and shall find
        ->    that I have created 4 new lines of data.
        ->    I will now enter two new lines of text
        ->    to see if it is accepted.
```

As we can see the header consists of the date and time, the page number, and the name of the file being printed. This header appears at the top of each page.

(2) The next example is to print the same file without the header being generated.

```
user    ->    pr -t letter<r>
UNIX    ->    This is a test to see if I am
        ->    entering text in the file ''letter''.
        ->    Once I have completed it and shall find
        ->    that I have created 4 new lines of data.
        ->    I will now enter two new lines of text
        ->    to see if it is accepted.
```

(3) The next example will use three files and print them out simultaneously, each in a column in the order they are named.

```
user    ->    pr -m file1 file2 file3<r>
UNIX    ->
        ->    Jan 6 19:17 1981 Page 1
```

1 line one	1 line one	1 line one
3 line three	3 line three	3 line three
7 line seven	6 line six	7 line seven
6 line six	2 line two	6 line six
2 line two	7 line seven	5 line five
5 line five	5 line five	2 line two
4 line four	4 line four	4 line four

$

(4) Now let's see how we can take advantage of the line count and the
     number of columns. We have seen that the "ls" command produces a
     single list of names for a given directory. By using the "pr" command
     with column and line arguments we can generate a multiple column
     list.

user   ->   ls|pr -5 -120<r>
UNIX   ->
           ->   Jan 6 19:18 1981 Page 1

AB	c	ch7.inf.fmt	chapt6	d
a	cat	ch7.stat	chapt6.fmt	dcheck
a.out	cc	ch7.stat.fmt	chgrp	dd
aa	ch5	chapt.fmt	chmod	debug
ab	ch5.1	chapt2	chown	df
ar	ch7.accn	chapt2.fmt	clri	diff
b	ch7.accn.fmt	chapt4	cmp	diff3
ba	ch7.bkup	chapt4.fmt	comm	file1
bb	ch7.bkup.fmt	chapt5	command	file1.c
book	ch7.inf	chapt5.fmt	cp	file1.o

$

     Notice that we used the ls command and a special symbol "|" to
get the list of names. This will be defined in the next chapter. In this
chapter we just want to concentrate on the specific commands themselves.

     We asked the pr command to produce 5 columns and limit the
number of lines to 20. This is so we can see a complete page on a crt.

     Summary:

     The pr command is generally used when a printout of the file or
files is required. As we saw from the previous examples we produced output
on our own terminal (standard output). One way in which to output to a
printer is by using the lpr command defined next.

5.5. Line Printer Spooler

Command:	lpr
Syntax:	lpr [option]. . . [file]. . .
Function:	This command allows you to print a file in the background while you are doing other things. The file(s) are placed in a queue and printed as the printer becomes available. This allows any user to request the printing of a file and not have to be concerned with others who may be requesting printouts at the same time.
Option:	The following options are available with the command. They are:

-r	Remove the file(s) after it has been queued.
-c	Copy the file to insulate against changes that may happen before printing.
-m	Report by mail(see chapter 7) when printing is complete.
-n	Do not report by mail(default).

Example:

(1) Send a file to the printer for printing and immediately give control back to allow the user to continue doing something else while the job is printing.

```
user   ->   lpr letter<r>
UNIX   ->   $
```

The lpr command has put the file in a queue and will print it whenever the printer is free. However the user is given control to continue doing whatever else is necessary.

(2) The user has several options available when printing. One is to remove the file being printed as soon as it has finished printing. This is generally used when the file has been generated only for this printing.

user   ->   lpr -r letter<r>
UNIX -> $

Once the file "letter" has been printed, the system will remove it. This is the same as if you had issued a "rm letter" command.

(3) The next example is just the opposite of the -r option. The -c option will allow you to start printing a file and immediately allow you to change it without affecting the file being printed.

user   ->   lpr -c letter<r>
UNIX -> $

In the previous examples the file was queued for printing, but if you had decided to continue editing(changing) it, the changes might have been reflected in the printed output. In this case a copy of the file is made for printing so that all new changes will not affect it.

Summary:

This command is very useful when you want to print something but do not want to see if the printer is busy or if you don't want to wait until the printing is complete before doing something else. Your file(s) are identified from others by your login name being printed on the first page of your output. Thus there is no need to wait at the printer for your output or have to identify it by the actual text printed.

5.6. Compare Two Files

Command:	cmp
Syntax:	cmp [-l][-s] file1 file2
Function:	The usage of this command is to compare two files and report any differences between them. It announces the byte and line number at which the difference occurred.
Option:	Two options exist that can alter the results of the compare.

-l	This option provides a complete list of the differences between the files. It prints (1) The position in the file (in decimal) of where the difference occurred. (2) The actual character(in octal)
-s	This option results in a return code based on the results of the compare. No other output is generated. If the two files were identical the return code is set to zero. For different files it is set to one and if the file(s) are inaccessible the return code is set to two.

Example:

(1) The simplest usage of the compare command is without the use of options. It will stop and print out the first occurrence of a difference between the two files. We have two files "aa and bb" which contain:

```
file aa      file bb
1 1 2 1 1    1 1 1 1 1
```

```
2 2 1 2 2    2 2 2 2 2
```

Notice that the differences are line 1 column 3 and line 2 column 3.

```
user   ->    cmp aa bb <r>
UNIX   ->    aa bb differ: char 3, line 1
       ->    $
```

As we stated before, only the first occurrence is printed.

(2) In this case we will use the option "-l". We can then see the exact location of each difference and the actual characters that are different.

```
user   ->    cmp -l aa bb <r>
UNIX   ->    5 62 61
       ->    15 61 62
       ->    $
```

We can see that in this case the position in the file is relative to the beginning of the file for each difference. Thus position 15 is the same as line 2 column 5. The octal representation of the actual characters themselves must be decoded.

Summary:

The option "-s" does not produce any output other than return codes and is generally used in conjunction with other commands in what we call shell files which will be reviewed in chapter 8. It should also be pointed out that when comparing two files using the "-l" option , the differences reported could be very large.

5.7. Remove Files

Command: rm

Syntax: rm [options] file. . .

Function: This function removes one or more files from a
                       directory. A file can only be removed if the user
                       issuing the rm command has write permission in
                       that directory. Read/write permission on the file
                       being deleted is not required.

Option: Three options exist for this command. They are:

-f   This option is useful only when a file does not have
                       read/write permission. Under normal conditions
                       when a file does not have read/write permission,
                       the system asks if the file should be deleted. If
                       the user responds "y", the file is deleted. The -f
                       option forces all files regardless to be deleted. The
                       "y" is never asked.

-r   This option allows all files and sub- directories to
                       be deleted.

-i   This option allows the user to interactively delete
                       files.

Example:

(1) Since we have already seen the basic format of the remove, we will
look at the options available in these examples. The first is the ability
to remove everything below a directory level. For example if we had
a structure as shown in figure 4.1, we could remove all of the files and
directories below the user root by use of the option "-r". We must first
position ourselves to the user root directory (or whereever we want to
start removing).

```
user   ->   rm -r *<r>
UNIX   ->   $
```

The "*" is a special symbol that indicates remove everything within the directory currently positioned at, including all subdirectories (more on this in the next chapter). This single command with the -r option will remove everything but the user root directory.

(2) Now let's see how we can interactively remove files. This may be useful when we have a lot of files in a directory and want to delete many of them. Rather than enter each name, we can use the interactive option "-i", and the system will provide the file names and all we have to do is state "y" for "yes" delete the file, or "n" for "no" don't delete the file.

```
user  ->   rm -i *<r>
UNIX  ->   file1:
user  ->   y<r>
UNIX  ->   file2:
.     ->
.     ->
.     ->
UNIX  ->   $
```

As we can see from this example the system gives us each name and we decide if we want to delete it or not. Again the "*" is used to specify all files in this directory.

Summary:

We demonstrated the value of the remove command in chapter 4; however, as you can see we have expanded it to the point that it could be very dangerous if not used properly. Thus before using it you should always be aware of the directory that you are in and certain that the pattern you are using is correct. The time that it takes to do this will be rewarded many times over by not having to go to backup tapes to recover things you accidentally deleted.

5.8. Find Files

Command:	find
Syntax:	find pathname. . . option. . .
Function:	The find command recursively descends the directory hierarchy for each pathname in the starting pathname provided and looks for files that match the options provided. For those options providing a value, such as number of days, etc., a plus sign(+) means more than and a minus sign (-) means less than. Any number of pathnames and options can be given in a single command just so long as it is consistent.
Option:	Each option is preceded by a minus sign ($-$). There is no order required other than a logical order to you. Multiple options are assumed to be AND'd, that is to say they all must be true for the complete statement to be true. A logical OR can be used for alternative options and is specified by a "-o". Parentheses must be "escaped", that is to say that a "\" must precede both the "(" and ")". The options are:

-name filename	True if this filename matches the current file name.
-type c	True if the type of the file is c for character file.
-links n	True if the file has n links.
-user uname	True if the file belongs to the user (login name or numeric user ID).
-group gname	True if the file belongs to a group (group name or numeric group ID).

-size n	True if the file is n blocks long.
-inum n	True if the file has inode number n.
-atime n	True if the file has been accessed in n days.
-mtime n	True if the file has been modified in n days.
-exec command	Executes a UNIX command. True if executed command returns a zero.
-ok command	Like the -exec command except that the generated command is written on the standard output, then the standard input is read and the command executed only upon response y.
-print	Always true; causes the current pathname to be printed (when condition is met).
-newer file	True if the current file has been modified more recently than the argument file.

Example:

(1) The most common use of this command is to locate a file when the number of directories is too large to manually search. Let's say that we would like to see if there are any files named a.out in the author's directories. To accomplish this we need only say:

```
user   ->   find /rp3/dick -name a.out -print <r>
UNIX   ->   /rp3/dick/unixbk/a.out
       ->   $
```

We were able to find one occurrence of the file "a.out". Notice that the complete pathname is printed. Also without the "-print" option nothing would have been displayed. In this case "rp3" is the root of a file system and the directory "dick" is the author's root directory. We could, if need be, search more than one root directory by placing them before or after the pathname "/rp3/dick" leaving one space between them (i.e.,/rp3/dick /rp3/sam /rp3/karen...).

(2) Another example is the use of the "find" command during maintenance of the system. We could run out of space and not know why it happened. Sometimes this is because one or more very large files were generated. The reason could be on purpose or accidentally. To correct this the system administrator must first determine the reasons for the overflow. This can sometimes be accomplished by use of the find command. For example we can say:

```
user   ->   find / -size +50 -mtime -1 -print <r>
UNIX  ->   /rp3/dick/unixbk/ar
       ->   $
```

We have asked to see a list of all the files that are greater than 50 blocks (512 bytes/block) and were created in the last 24 hours. There is only one entry in this example; however, there could be many of them. If this was the case, you would have to see which ones caused the problem if any.

(3) Yet another use of the find command is to locate and delete files that are no longer required. A case in point is the object modules "*.o" that are created when the c compiler is run. To delete these files we can execute the find command and then remove each file manually, or we can do it in the find command itself.

```
user   ->   find / -name '*.o' -print <r>
UNIX  ->   /rp3/dick/working/prog1.o
       ->   /rp3/dick/unixbk/file1.o
       ->   /rp3/dick/unixbk/tbl.o
       ->   /rp3/dick/yard/test1.o
       ->   /rp3/dick/mbox.o
       ->   $
```

This command generated only a list of the ".o" files. We would then have to delete each of them using the remove (rm) command. However we can remove them at the same time we are finding them by using the -exec option. We simply say:

```
user   ->   find / -name '*.o' -exec rm\; <r>
UNIX  ->   $
```

The $ indicates that all ".o" files have been removed. In this example we did not know the names of all the ".o" files and were able to use the "*" just as we would in any UNIX command to indicate that anything coming before the ".o" was not important.

Summary:

This command is useful to anyone who has to find one or more specific files and doesn't know what directory(s) to start looking in. It is very useful to the system administrator who must keep the necessary free space available, but maintain the file system when something goes wrong.

5.9. Archive and Library Maintainer

Command: ar

Syntax: ar option [posname] archive_file [file1. . .]

Function: The ar command is issued to save or store groups of files into a single archive file. It provides the capability to create, add, extract, list, move, and delete files from/to an archive file.

Option: Several options exist each of which is represented as an option to the ar command and perform the following tasks.

d   Delete the named files from the archive file.

r	Replace the named files in the archive file. If the files does not exist, the new file is added.
q	Quickly append the named files to the end of the archive file. No check is performed to determine if the file already exists.
t	Prints a table of contents of the archive file.
p	Prints the contents of the selected files.
m	Moves the named files to the end of the archive file or if posname is given, moves to indicated position.
x	Extract the named files, Does not alter the archive file.

The following options are used in conjunction with the other options.

v	Verbose-when used with d,r,q,m,x, prints the function performed and the file name.
c	Create archive file. Normally archive file is automatically created.
l	Used with any option, will place the archive temp files in a local directory.
a	Used with r or m specifies that the named file is to be placed after the file indicated by the posname.
b	Same as a except that placement is before.
u	Used with r, indicates that only those files with modified dates later than the archive files are replaced.

Example:

(1) Adding new files to an existing or non existing archive file can be accomplished by using the r option. Let's say we have four files named a,b,c,d. We can add them to an archive file by simply saying:

user   –>   ar rv library a b c d <r>
UNIX   –>   a - a
         –>   a - b

```
->    a - c
->    a - d
->    ar: creating library
->    $
```

We can see that this is a new library by the fact that the message "ar: creating library" appears. If the library already existed we would not get this message. The use of the v option is to let us know what is happening. It's probably a good idea to use it (at least at first). It defines the function performed "a = add" followed by the name of the file.

(2) Next we replace an existing file in the library with a new one. To do this we use the same command format.

```
user  ->    ar rv library b  <r>
UNIX  ->    r - b
      ->    $
```

Notice that in this case we did not create a new library, but only used an existing one. The file "b" in library was replaced by the new file "b".

(3) There may be times when we would like more than one copy of a file in the library at the same time. We add a file to the end of the library by using the q option.

```
user  ->    ar qv library a  <r>
UNIX  ->    q - a
      ->    $
```

There will now exist two copies of the file a.

(4) At some time we will want to get a list of all names of the files in our library. To do this we use the option t.

```
user  ->    ar t library  <r>
```

```
UNIX  ->    a
      ->    b
      ->    c
      ->    d
      ->    a
      ->    $
```

In this case we did not have to name the files. As we can see from the previous function we have two copies of the file "a".

(5) We can also print the contents of selected files by using the option p. Note that if we do not enter any names the contents of all files will be printed. In this case we may want to direct the output to another file.

```
user  ->    ar p library b >/dev/lp
UNIX  ->    $
```

The contents of file b in the archive file "library" is extracted and directed towards the printer. The use of ">" for I/O direction is explained in chapter 6, but for now we are interested only in the archive functions.

(6) There will also be times when we require a file to be extracted from an archive file. By using the option x we can do this.

```
user  ->    ar xv library b c <r>
UNIX  ->    x - b
      ->    x - c
      ->    $
```

The archive file has not been affected and the two files b and c have been placed in the current directory. If no file names had been given, all files in the archive file would have been extracted.

(7) We can delete any or all files in an archive file by use of the option d. Once they have been deleted they can only be replaced by the same file from outside the archive file.

user   —>   ar dv library a <r>
UNIX —>   d – a
        —> $

     The first occurence of "a" was deleted in this case. If you re-member we added a file a to the end of the archive library earlier. Thus we only deleted the first copy of it. To delete the next copy we must perform the function over again.

(8) In an earlier example we saw that we could add to the end of an archive file by using the option q. We can also move files around within an archive file by the use of the option m. By itself it will always move the named file to the end of the archive file. How-ever we can move a file before or after another file by use of the options a or b appended to the option m. The option u is used for conditional replacement based on the modified dates of the files. To move file a (currently at the end of the archive file) to the front of the archive file we need only give the following command using the following data base.

    b
    c
    d   - existing files in library and their order
    a

user   —>   ar mbv b library a <r>
UNIX —>   m – a
        —> $

     The new order of the library will be

    a
    b
    c
    d

Summary:

We cannot possibly show all of the ways one can use the command ar. You must create your own archive file and just experiment. You can start with the files and functions shown here.

5.10. Change Mode

Command: chmod

Syntax: chmod option file . . .

Function: The chmod command allows us to change the read, write, execute permissions on one or more files. Refer back to the "ls" command for details on the permissions for a file.

Option: The options come in two forms, the first being an octal representation of the permissions, and the second being a symbolic representation. The octal mode requires that your specify the entire set of changes for a file. In other words you are not allowed to change one condition, without affecting the others. The octal mode is simply an octal number constructed from the logical ORing of the following modes.

o 4000 set execution mode for user (login name or ID)
o 2000 set execution mode for group (group name or ID)
o 1000 sticky bit, not read, write, execute permissions
o 0400 user (login name) read permission
o 0200 user (login name) write permission
o 0100 user (login name) execute permission

o 0070 group read,write,execute permission
o 0007 all others read,write,execute permission

The symbolic mode has the form:

chmod [ugoa][+-=][rwxstugo] file...
where:
[who] op permission[op permission]...
Takes on the form:

who = [ugoa]

u = user(login name)
g = group
o = others
a = user,group,others(default)

op = +(for add permission)
-(for delete permission)

permission = [rwxstugo]

r = read
w = write
x = execute
s = set owner or group id
t = save text - sticky
ugo = permission to be taken from
the current mode.

Example:

(1) One of the simplest ways to protect your files from destruction by other people is to write protect them. Let's say that the file "file1" used in previous examples is to be protected from others. The current setting of permissions for file1 can be seen be issuing a "ls -l file1" command:

    -rw-rw-rw- 1 dick 83 Oct 15 17:03 file1

The current mode is read-write for everyone. To change it

```
user   ->    chmod 0644 file1 <r>
or     ->
user   ->    chmod go-w file1 <r>
UNIX   ->    $
```

We can see the results by using the "ls -l file1"

```
UNIX   ->    -rw-r--r-- 1 dick     83 Oct 15 17:03 file1
       ->    $
```

The results are the same using the octal mode or the symbolic mode. Which one you use is up to you. In the octal case we stated that the 6 was read,write permission for the user(login name) and 44 was for read only for group and others. In the symbolic case we stated that go was group and others and to turn the write permission off for both of them(-w).

(2) There are times when we will want to make a file executable (see chapter 8, making shell files). Again we can do this by using the octal or the symbolic modes. To make the file "file1" executable we simply say:

```
user   ->    chmod 0755 file1 <r>
or     ->
user   ->    chmod a+x file1 <r>
UNIX   ->    $
```

By issuing a "ls -l file1" we can see the permissions.

```
UNIX   ->    -rwxr-xr-x 1 dick     83 Oct 15 17:03 file1
       ->    $
```

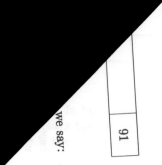

made the file "file1" executable. The octal
r to have read, write, execute permission
only read and execute permission.

seful when used properly. Be careful that
that you cannot access the file yourself.
...s a good habit to check the changes by using the "ls" command after
each change to be sure that they are correct.

5.11. Change Owner

Command: chown

Syntax: chown owner file. . .

Function: This command allows you to change the ownership
                   of one or more files to a specific owner(login name).
                   To change ownership you must be the owner of the
                   file or be the superuser.

Option: No options exist for this command.

Example:

(1) Since there is only one format we will show it. We will take a file
    owned by dick and change it to another owner(login name). Again we
    will use the file "file1" as our example. Its current format is:

     -rwxr-xr-x 1 dick 83 Oct 15 17:03 file1

        The current owner is dick as seen above. Now let's issue the chown
commmand.

```
user    ->    chown darrin file1 <r>
```

```
UNIX  ->   $
```

Now to see the results we issue a "ls -l file1" command.

```
UNIX  ->   -rwxr-xr-x 1 darrin    83 Oct 15 17:03 file1
      ->   $
```

As we can see the only thing that has changed is the owner from dick to darrin. Remember that the new owner must be a legal login name; otherwise, the owner will not change.

Summary:

This command is necessary to the system administrator who must set up new login names and directories in addition to other requirements. The average user will probably not have that much need for it; however, there may be times when it will be useful.

5.12. Change Group

Command:	chgrp
Syntax:	chgrp group file. . .
Function:	This command allows you to change a group of one or more files to a specific group(group name). To change group you must be in the same group for a file or be the superuser.
Option:	No options exist for this command.

Example:(change group ownership)

(1) Since there is only one format, we will show it. We will take a file in the group root and change it to another group(group name). Again we will use the file "file1" as our example. Its current format is:

-rwxr-xr-x 1 dick 83 Oct 15 17:03 file1

The current group is 1 as seen above. Now let's issue the chgrp commmand.

user   ->   `chgrp 2 file1 <r>`
UNIX ->   `$`

Now to see the results we issue a "ls -l file1" command.

-rwxr-xr-x 2 darrin 83 Oct 15 17:03 file1 $

As we can see the only thing that has changed is the group, from 1 to 2. Remember that the new group must be a legal group name, otherwise, the group will not change.

Summary:

This command is necessary to the system administrator who must set up new login names and directories in addition to groups. The average user will probably not have that much need for it; however, there will be times when it will be useful. It is more useful to the average user than is the chown command because it is more likely one will change groups from time to time.

5.13. Questions

Using the following files and directories, answer questions 1-4.

```
file1          file2
1 1 1 1 1 1    2 2 2 2 2 2
1 1 1 1 1 1    2 2 2 2 2 2
```

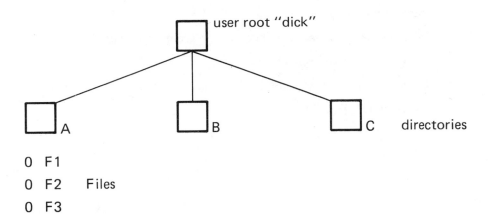

figure 5.1

(1) Show the results of the following commands:

    a) cat file1 file2

    b) cat file1 file2 > file3

    c) cat > file4

(2) Describe how the following command works and when it should be used:

    lpr file1

(3) Describe the function of the command "pr" and when you might use it.

(4) Describe the resulting file structure and where you are positioned after each of the following commands:

    a) login dick

    b) cd A

    c) cp F1 ../B

    d) cd ../

    e) cp A/F2 B/FA

    f) cp A B

    g) mv B C

    h) mv C/FA B/F1

(5)   What are the change owner and change group commands?

      Why would you want to use them?

(6)   Describe the results of the following commands:

    a) chmod 0755 file1

    b) chmod 0664 file2

    c) chmod 0700 file1

    d) chmod 0644 file2

6. Introduction to the UNIX Shell

The UNIX shell is both a command language and a programming language that provides an interface to the UNIX operating system. This chapter will deal with some of the simple things needed to increase the capability for each of your UNIX commands. Up to this point we have described several UNIX commands. However, in each case the input to the system and the output from the system were controlled by the system (refered to as standard input and standard output). If you remember, for the commands "pwd" and "ls" the input was the command itself, and the output was information obtained by the system and directed back to your terminal.

Standard input/output unless otherwise changed by the user is (input) from the terminal and (output) back to the terminal. There are going to be times when you will want the input/output direction changed (going to and coming from) to a place other than the terminal.

6.1. Input/Output Redirection

To direct input/output from your terminal to another media, you can use the symbols "<,<<,>,>>". The symbol "<" is used to direct the input from a file to a command or another file.

Example:

Let's say that we have a file that contains a list of directories that we are going to sort in reverse order. This file is called "dir" and contains the names "A B C". We can then say:

```
user   ->   sort -r < dir<r>
UNIX   ->   C
       ->   B
       ->   A
       ->   $
```

As we can see from this command, the file "dir" is used as the input instead of your terminal. Each command defaults to the standard input(your terminal) unless you direct it elsewhere. In this case we are directing the input by use of the symbol "<".

Let's now see what we do to direct the output to a file instead of your terminal. In this case we use the symbol ">" to indicate that the output is to be placed somewhere else.

Example:

Place the output from the "ls" command in a file called lsout.

```
user   ->   ls -l > lsout<r>
UNIX   ->   $
user   ->   cat lsout<r>          display contents of file
UNIX   ->   A
       ->   B
       ->   C
       ->   $
```

Notice that the output from the file looks exactly like that which would have been displayed directly on your terminal. The difference is that it is more permanent. We can now call it up and use it anytime we like. If the file lsout already existed, we would replace the previous contents with the new contents. However if we want to keep the existing contents and just add this new data to it we can simply use the output directive ">>".

Example:

Place the output from the "ls" command in the file lsout(adding to the previous contents).

The current file "lsout" looks as follows:

A
B
C

```
user   ->    ls >> lsout<r>
UNIX   ->    $
user   ->    cat lsout<r>          display contents of file
UNIX   ->    A
       ->    B
       ->    C
       ->    A
       ->    B
       ->    C
       ->    $
```

As we can see from this example we have just added this list to the end of the identical list previously generated.

6.2. Background Commands

There may be times when you would like to run a program or UNIX command without having to wait until it finishes before doing something else. This can be accomplished by use of the symbol "&" added to the end of the command.

Example:(Run UNIX program in the background)

If we want to get a list of file and directory names and place them in another file "dir", but while we're doing it we would like to start editing yet a third file, we would say:

```
user   ->    ls > dir&<r>
UNIX   ->    165              this is the process number
       ->    $                you can now start your edit
user   ->    ed letter<r>
UNIX   ->     271
       ->                     ready to start editing
```

What we have done is to start the "ls" command running and then immediately (before the "ls" finishes) start editing the file "letter". The UNIX system creates what is called a new process which runs the first command and gives control of the shell back to you so that you can continue doing something else. The number of processes that you can have running at the same time is limited by the UNIX system itself and if that limit has been exceeded a message will be given. More information will be provided about processes later.

Remember that not all commands can run in the background. It is not difficult to determine which ones can and which ones cannot be executed as background processes. For example it would make no sense to run the editor in the background mode when you are trying to edit a file.

6.3. Pipes and filters

We have discussed how to redirect the input and output of a command. Now we will look at how we can pass data generated by one command to another. This is accomplished by the use of the symbol "|":

Example:

Get the directory and file names using the "ls" command and pass the results to the sort routine which will sort the names in reverse order and write it out to the standard output(your terminal)

```
user     ->    ls -l | sort -r<r>
```

```
UNIX  ->   C
      ->   B
      ->   A
      ->   $
```

This is the same as if we had said:

```
user  ->   ls -l >file1; sort -r <file1<r>
UNIX  ->   C
      ->   B
      ->   A
      ->   $
```

Notice that we can write more than one command on a single line by separating them with the symbol ";". This is the same as if we had written each command as:

```
user  ->   ls -l >file1<r>
UNIX  ->   $
user  ->   sort -r < file1<r>
UNIX  ->   C
      ->   B
      ->   A
      ->   $
```

The only difference between these two examples is that the second example requires a temporary file "file1". The first example uses what we call a pipeline between the two commands that allows the data generated by the "ls" command to be directed to the second command "sort"; thus the temporary file is not needed. If we needed the data generated by the first command at a later time then it would be more practical to use the temporary file. Pipes are useful when the data is to be used only by another command right away and then discarded.

A filter is a command that reads its standard input, transforms it in some way, and prints the result as output. The sort command is a filter in that it accepts the standard input, sorts it according to the arguments provided by you and outputs the results.

For example, the previous example used the sort command to accept data from the ls command and then output it in a selected order.

6.4. Use of Metacharacters

Many of the commands accept arguments which are the names of files.

For example:

user   ->   `ls -l /usr/dick/file1<r>`

Prints information about the file "file1" as previously defined.

The shell provides a mechanism for generating a list of file names that match a pattern. The first such symbol that can be used for matching is "*". This symbol used by itself says that all entries are to be selected, and when used with part of a name it allows you to select all names that match that pattern.

Example:

user   ->   `ls -l /usr/dick/fil*<r>`

This command will select all names that start with "fil". The remaining characters are ignored in the selection process. The "*" can be used anywhere in a name and if necessary more than once.

user   ->   `ls -l /usr/dick/*e1<r>`

This pattern will select all names that end in "e1".

```
user   ->   ls -l /usr/dick/*aa*<r>
```

This pattern will select all names that have an aa somewhere in the name.

```
user   ->   ls -l /usr/dick/f*e1<r>
```

This pattern will select all names that start with "f" and end with "e1".

The use of "*" indicates that one or more characters are involved. Many times you will want to find names that are similar except for one character in a particular position. In this case you can use the symbol "?". Whereever it appears in a name, it means that that exact position in the name is to be ignored.

Example:

```
user   ->   ls -l file?<r>
```

This pattern will select all the names that start with file and have only one additional character. The last character can be any legal character. For example "file1, file2, filex" are all patterns that would be selected by this command. The "?" can appear more than once and anywhere in a name.

```
user   ->   ls -l f?le?<r>
```

This pattern will select all the names that start with "f", followed by any single character, followed by the letters "le", and ending with any single character.

As with the "*", used by itself it will select everything, whereas the "?" used by itself will select all names that have only a single character. The files "A,B,C" for example would be selected.

We can also select names based on a range of values. This is accomplished by entering the values in the range in a set of brackets "[]".

Example:

    user   ->   ls -l [a-z]*<r>

This pattern will select all names that start with a letter a to z followed by any number of other characters. Thus we could select the names "axxy23,cer5t,z,etc".

The symbols we have just defined ($<$ $>$ * ? fi &) are called metacharacters and have a special meaning to the shell as we have just described. However there may be times when we want to use these characters in a name. We can accomplish this by inserting the symbol "\" just before the metacharacter. If we use more than one metacharacter in a name we need one "\" for each metacharacter.

Example:

    user   ->   ls -l file\?<r>

The ? is literally interpreted as the character "?" and the file name is "file?". No pattern search is created in this case.

    user   ->   ls -l f*le\?<r>

This command selects only the name "f*le?".

6.5. Summary

In this chapter we have learned how to (1) redirect our input/output, (2) run commands in the background, (3) use pipes and filters, and (4) use metacharacters to select names based on a pattern. There are too many commands to show exactly how all of these features work on each of the commands so it is in your best interest to experiment with them. In most cases it will be obvious if a particular feature will or will not work. In all other cases you can just try it. It won't take you long to know when you can or cannot use them.

6.6. Questions

(1)   From where does UNIX expect your input and where does it place any output generated?

(2)   What is the procedure to direct data generated by a command to a file instead of your terminal?

(3)   What is the procedure to direct data to your command instead of from your terminal?

(4)   In UNIX terminology, define what a process is.

(5)   Can you have more than one process running at the same time?

　　　If yes, how can you do it?

(6)   Can you pass data from one command to another without using a temporary file? If yes, what is this procedure called, and how do you invoke it?

(7)   What are the special characters " * , ? " and what do they do?

(8)   What is the function performed by the following command:

　　　ls -l [a-z]*

7. UNIX Commands

7.1. Communications

Communications is a very important function in everyday life. In business it is even more important in that you are always having to communicate with someone. However the problems are much more difficult because of the timing. The difference of only a few minutes can be critical in making a decision. With the time changes around the world and the fact that everyone is not always where they are supposed to be, it is even more critical. Thus any means by which we can communicate in a way that is easy and yet assures us that the other party(s) will be able to get our message or contact us can be worth large amounts of money. The following commands provide the user with a means to communicate with the system and with other users.

7.1.1. Sending and Receiving Mail

Command: mail

Syntax:	mail [login name]. . .
	or
	mail [-r] [-q] [-p] [-f file]

Function: The mail command provides a user with the ability to read mail sent by others, in first-out or first-in order, and allow it to be printed. The user can also send mail to other users.

Option: Several options exist which may be used in conjunction with the mail command. They are:

-r	This option causes the messages to be ordered as first-in,first-out. If no option is provided, a last-in,first-out order is used.
-q	This option causes mail to exit after interrupt without changing the mailbox.
-p	This option causes the mail to be printed.
-f	This option causes the named file (mailbox) to be printed as if it were the mailbox.

Once you are reading your mail you have the ability to control it with the following options.

\<r\>	return key goes to new line
d	delete message and go on to the next
p	print message again
-	go back to previous message
s[file]. . .	Save the message in the named files (mailbox is default)
w[file]. . .	Save the message, without a header, in the named files (mailbox is default)

m[user name]. . .   Mail the message to the named persons (yourself is default)

EOT(control-D)   Put unexamined mail back in the mailbox and stop

q   Same as EOT

x   Exit, without changing the mailbox file

!   Escape to Shell to do another UNIX command

?   Print a summary of the commands

Example:

(1) When you first log into the system, it will inform you if you have any mail (i.e., someone has sent you mail). The system will appear as follows:

```
UNIX  ->   login:
user  ->   dick<r>
UNIX  ->   you have mail
      ->   $
```

At this point, to see the mail you simply enter the name "mail" with any of the options desired (-r,-q,-p) and strike the return key <r>. All messages sent to you since the last time you viewed your mail will be displayed.

The order will be determined by the option -r or no option. In this case let's say that three messages were sent.

```
user  ->   mail<r>
UNIX  ->
      ->     From Patricia Sat Jan 10 10:49:34 1981
      ->     this is the third message to be sent
      ->
      ->     From darrin Sat Jan 10 10:49:07 1981
      ->     This is the second message to be sent
      ->
      ->     From Roy Sat Jan 10 10:48:03 1981
```

```
->     This is the first of several messages
->     to be sent to dick.
->
->     save?
```

We can see from this example that the three messages are dated and time stamped and in this case outputted in order of last-in, first-out. Now let's see how we send mail to others.

(2) We will send a message to the three people that we received messages from. We will also send a message to ourself to see how it is handled.

user	->	mail patricia darrin roy dick<r>
UNIX	->	no response(waits for message)
user	>	This is to let you know that I received <r>
	->	your message and will follow up on it. <r>
	->	strike control-d keys
	->	to exit and send message.
UNIX	->	$

This message has now been sent to the four people named in the mail command above. When they login or request mail, they will be informed that mail has been sent to them. More than one message can be sent by you and/or others at different times. The system dates and time stamps each message and concatenates it to any other messages that have been sent. Thus when the user requests mail, all messages are displayed.

Remember the message we sent to ourself? We can view it by simply entering the command "mail". In fact for any mail that has been sent after we are logged into the system, we can view it by entering the mail command. There is no indication that mail was sent so we will have to check every now and then. If not, the mail will stay until the next time we login.

user	->	mail<r>
UNIX	->	From dick Sat Jan 10 11:21:23 1981

```
              ->    This is to let you know that I received<r>
              ->    your message and will follow up on it. <r>
              ->    save?
user          ->    y<r>                    "y" indicates save, "n" no
                                            save
UNIX  ->  $
```

As we can see from this example the system asks us if we want to save the message or not. If the answer is yes, we enter a "y" and return, otherwise any other response will result in the message(s) not being saved.

Any time during processing (after you have logged in) you may ask the system if any mail has been sent by entering the commmand "mail". If some has been sent the system will display your mail, however if no mail is sent the system will merely respond with the message "no mail".

```
user      ->    mail<r>
UNIX  ->    no mail
          ->    $
```

Summary:

This is a very useful command when you cannot see the individual in person and want to be assured that they will be informed.

You must remember that when sending messages you have to have the correct login name or the message may be sent to the wrong person or possibly not sent at all.

7.1.2. Write to All Users

Command: wall

Syntax: wall

Function: This command is generally issued by the systems administrator when everyone on the system must be notified of some upcoming event such as no disk space, hardware failure (tape drive, printer, etc.).

Option: There are no options for this command.

Example:

(1) Send a message to all users that the computer will be unavailable until further notice.

```
user   ->    wall<r>
       ->    The computer will be down for about one
       ->    hour.  Please logoff.
       ->                         control-"d" to send message
UNIX  ->     Broadcast Message .  .  .
       ->    The computer will be down for about one
       ->    hour.  Please logoff.
```

Summary:

As we stated before, this command is very useful when all users must be immediately notified. The message is sent to only those people who are currently logged into the system. However, others will receive messages when they log in.

7.1.3. Write to Another User

Command: write

Syntax: write user [ttyname]

Function: This command allows you to write to another user
                         who is currently logged into the system. You can
                         then talk to each other by the use of this com-
                         mand. You must set up a protocol so that the
                         messages being sent back and forth are not inter-
                         mixed. This can be accomplished in a number of
                         ways similar to those used on CB's and other one
                         way radios. If you do not want to have messages
                         interrupt you during some task, you can deny mes-
                         sages by use of the command "mesg".

Option: NO options exist for this command.

Example:

(1) You are logged in as "dick" and will write to the user whose login name
     is "darrin".

     dick's input:


```
user    ->    write darrin<r>
UNIX    ->                          no response, awaits for mes-
                                    sage to be entered
  .     ->
  .     ->
  .     ->
        ->    darrin's terminal:
UNIX    ->    message from dick tty1
```

Darrin can then wait for the message from dick or enter "write dick".
One must be careful not to overwrite the other's message being entered.
This requires a protocol that will insure that a message is not sent at the
same time the other user is entering a message to be sent. A simple protocol
that will allow each user to know when the other is sending or waiting to
receive is as follows:

                              - when you receive a message "message from —
                              tty?"

- you wait until you receive the first message with a "o" at the end. This will indicate that its your turn to respond.

- each time either of you want a response from the other, issue a "o" at the end of the last line of your message.

- when you are finished, you can issue a "oo" to indicate that you are signing off.

How you set up a protocol is not important as long as each of you understand what it is and how it works.

Now let's continue with our example. Once you have issued the command you can start entering your message. Each time you strike the return key <r>you will send that line to the other person.

dick responds(after issuing the write)

```
user   ->    This is to let you know that I am <r>
       ->    working on project x and will be done <r>
       ->    with the specification by tomorrow.  oo<r>
.      ->
.      ->
.      ->
```

Input to darrin's terminal

```
UNIX  ->    This is to let you know that I am
      ->    working on project x and will be done
      ->    with the specification by tomorrow.  oo
      ->    EOF
      ->    $
```

As we can see from this example, the date entered by dick is exactly the same as that sent to darrin. Although it is not shown in this example, if we had not used the protocol shown earlier, and darrin had started entering a message at the same time dick was sending his, the message would have overlapped with the text being entered by darrin.

Summary:

This command, unlike the mail command, allows you to correspond with another person logged into the system immediately opposed to waiting until the other user asks for mail. Sometimes, if the message is long, you can use the mail to send it and then use the write command to tell the other user that (s)he has mail. Again remember about setting up some kind of protocol.

7.1.4. Permit or Deny Messages

Command: mesg

Syntax: mesg [n] [y]

Function: This command allows you to permit others to write to you or deny them permission to write to you. There will be times when you do not want others to write to you and interfere with what you are doing.

Option: There are two options which, when used with this command, allow you to control other users writing to you. The first option, "n", allows you to deny others from writing to you. This option will remain in effect as long as you are logged in or until you use the "y" option to allow others to write to you. The second option "y" is as we just stated; that is, it will allow others to write to you at any time. The default is that the system will allow others to write to you.

Example:

(1)   Let's say you are about to do an edit and do not want anyone to write a message to you until you have completed it. All you have to do is:

```
user    ->    mesg n<r>
UNIX  ->    $
```

At this point no other users can write to you. If they try, the system will send them a message telling them that they cannot write to you.

Then, just as soon as you are finished with the editing you should enter the mesg command to allow others to write to you. Since there may be a very good reason for sending you a message and you do not want to miss it.

```
user    ->    mesg y<r>
UNIX  ->    $
```

At this point you have set the conditions so that others may write to you.

Summary:

You should learn to use this command with caution. It is probably not in your best interest to have it set to deny others writing to you. So again use it with caution. Remember that once you log out and then log back in the option will be set to allow others to write to you.

7.1.5. Questions

(1) Can mail be sent to more than one person at a time?

(2) Can several people send you mail while you are not on the system?

(3) When does the UNIX system tell you that you have mail?

(4) If there is a problem with the system, is there any way to automatically inform all the current users on the system?

(5) when writing to another user, when is the message sent and when is it received?

(6)   Who can you write to?

7.2. Information Handling Commands

The need to perform small but important functions when dealing with your files is unavoidable. However without the proper tools to perform these functions, it can become a very difficult if not impossible task. UNIX is one of those systems that provides a wealth of tools that can make life much more bearable.

The following commands are used by all users when dealing with the selection and gathering of information about files and directories.

7.2.1. Select or Reject Lines Common to Two Files

Command: comm

Syntax: comm [-[123]] file1 file2

Function: The usage of this command is to select or reject lines that are common to two sorted files. A three column output is produced based on the options which can include:

o   lines different only in file1
o   lines different only in file2
o   lines identical in both files

Option: The options "123" represent the columns that are displayed. Including one or more of the options will result in the corresponding column being suppressed(not printed). Thus the option "-1" would result in the differences for the first file to be suppressed. The option "-12" would result in the differences for both files being suppressed. i.e., the only printout would be the lines identical in both files.

Example:

(1) The simplest usage is just to compare two sorted files using no options. Thus for the two files:

```
sfile1              sfile2
1 line one          1 line one
2 line two          2 line two
3 line three        3 line three
4 line four         4 line four
5 line five         5 line five
6 line six          6 line six
7 line seven        7 line seven
```

We can enter the command:

```
user   ->    comm sfile1 sfile2 <r>
UNIX   ->            1 line one
       ->            2 line two
       ->    3 line three
       ->        3 line three     .
       ->            4 line four
       ->            5 line five
       ->            6 line six
       ->            7 line seven
       ->    $
```

We can see by the results of this compare that there exist three columns of output. Their meaning is:

o   Column 1 shows the lines in sfile1 that are different from sfile2.

o   Column 2 shows the lines in sfile2 that are different from sfile1.

o   Column 3 displays the lines that are identical in sfile1 and sfile2.

(2) Now we can start using the options to display only the columns of output that we want. First by using any one of the options by themselves will result in the suppression of the printing for that option. Thus the command:

```
user   ->    comm -1 sfile1 sfile2 <r>
UNIX  ->            1 line one
      ->            2 line two
      ->    3 line three
      ->            4 line four
      ->            5 line five
      ->            6 line six
      ->            7 line seven
      ->    $
```

As can be seen from this example the differences for the file "sfile1" are not printed. If we were to use the option -2 or -3 then those columns would not be printed.

(3) We can also use combinations of the options. This will allow us to print only those columns we actually want. In the previous example we saw that we could only suppress one column at a time. However if we want to suppress two columns we simply use the option numbers representing those columns we want suppressed. To produce only the differences for sfile1 we would say:

```
user   ->    comm -23 sfile1 sfile2 <r>
```

```
UNIX  ->    3 line three
      ->    $
```

We can even suppress all three columns by using the option -123; however, the results would be meaningless.

Summary:

The syntax for this command is the same as the others. We can also direct the results (output) to another file or command.

7.2.2. Convert and Copy a File

Command:	dd
Syntax:	dd [option-value]. . .
Function:	This command provides the capability to specify input and output files and various conversion and copy options. Some of its usefulness is in dealing with tape of different formats, EBCDIC and ASCII formats, upper and lower case characters blocking, etc.
Option:	Many options exist which can be used together.

The options are:

if=	input file name.
of=	output file name.
ibs=n	input block size n bytes(default 512)
obs=n	output block size n bytes-(def 512)
bs=n	set both ip/op block size
cbs=n	conversion buffer size
skip=n	skip n input records before copy

files=n	copy n files from (tape) input
seek=n	seek n rec's from beginning of
	output file before copying
count=n	copy only n input records

The next option contains several suboptions and is useful when transferring data between different computers.

– conv =	
ascii	convert EBCDIC to ASCII
ebcdic	convert ASCII to EBCDIC
ibm	slightly different map of ASCII
	to EBCDIC
lcase	map alphabetics to lower case
ucase	map alphabetics to upper case
swap	swap every pair of bytes
noerror	do not stop processing on an error
sync	pad every input record to ibs
.. , ..	several comma-separated conversions

Example:

(1) A simple case of outputting blocked data or inputting blocked data. Output data blocked 16 blocks to a record

   user   –>   dd of=/dev/rmt0 bs=16b. .   .   .   .   .

Input data blocked 16 blocks to a record

   user   –>   dd if=/dev/rmt0 bs=16b. .   .   .   .

In both these cases raw I/O is specified where /dev/rmt0 happens to be the name of a tape unit. The block size is obvious; however, you must remember to include the b after the block size number.

(2) Next we may want to convert all alphabetic data in a file to upper case letters. This can be done by use of the option conv=ucase. Lets take the file "file1" and convert it to upper case letters. The current file "file1" contains:

```
1 line one
3 line three
7 line seven
6 line six
2 line two
5 line five
4 line four
```

To convert it to upper case letters we enter:

```
user   ->   dd if=file1 of=ab conv=ucase <r>
UNIX   ->   1 LINE ONE
       ->   3 LINE THREE
       ->   7 LINE SEVEN
       ->   6 LINE SIX
       ->   2 LINE TWO
       ->   5 LINE FIVE
       ->   4 LINE FOUR
       ->   $
```

Only the alphabetics will be converted to upper case. We could have left the option "of=ab" off and the standard I/O would have been used, which in this case is to the terminal.

(3) Another useful option is the "conv=swab". The PDP-11 series computers reverse the order of the bytes in a word. And although this is not noticeable to the user of a PDP-11 computer it is a problem when moving data to another 16 bit computer that doesn't reverse

the order(and most others don't). When swapping the order of bytes
between computers, a file with the bytes reversed looks as:


```
1ILENO EN3
L NI EHTER
E 7ILENS VENE6
L NI EIS
X 2ILENT OW5
L NI EIFEV4
L NI EOFUR
```


To convert it to the correct format can be done as:


```
user   ->    dd if=ba conv=swab <r>
UNIX   ->    1 LINE ONE
       ->    3 LINE THREE
       ->    7 LINE SEVEN
       ->    6 LINE SIX
       ->    2 LINE TWO
       ->    5 LINE FIVE
       ->    4 LINE FOUR
```


Summary:

As we can see by these examples the usefulness of this command is in
the handling of data between computers where formats are different.

7.2.3. Differences Between Two Files

Command: diff

Syntax: diff [-efbh] file1 file2

Function:	This command defines the changes that must be made in two files in order to bring them into agreement(look exactly alike). This capability can provide you with the methodology to keep backup copies of files without having to keep the total contents of each file.
Option:	Four options exist that provide additional capabilities for the differential file comparator. These are:
-e	This option is the most important in that it produces a set of difference commands that are compatible with the ed editor, thus providing a means in which to upgrade a file out of match with another.
-b	This option causes all trailing blanks (spaces and tabs) to be ignored and other strings of blanks to compare equal.
-f	This option produces a script of differences similar to that of the -e option,but not useful with ed.
-h	This option is much faster, but does not do as good a job of finding all the differences.

Example:

(1) A simple usage of the diff command is to find out just what the differences are. This can be done with the two files:

file1	file2
1 line one	1 line one
3 line three	3 line three
7 line seven	6 line six
6 line six	2 line two
2 line two	7 line seven
5 line five	5 line five
4 line four	4 line four

Then executing the command:

```
user   ->   diff file1 file2 <r>
UNIX   ->   3d2
       ->   < 7 line seven
       ->   5a5
       ->   > 7 line seven
       ->   $
```

We can see that by simply deleting line 7 of file1 (third line) and adding a new line (same as line 7 just deleted) just after line 5, we can make file1 look exactly like file2. Although the two files on first glance look quite different, they are actually quite similar.

(2) There are times when you would like to back off from a file and reconstruct an older one from the new one without having to do it by hand. This can be accomplished by using the -e option which finds the differences just as the previous example, but produces output acceptable to the ed editor. Again using the same files as shown above, we can demonstrate the results.

```
user   ->   diff -e file1 file2 <r>
UNIX   ->   5a
       ->   7 line seven
       ->   .
       ->   3d
       ->   $
```

This output can now be run through the ed editor and update file1 so that it will look exactly like file2.

Summary:

This is a very useful tool when the need arises to keep backup copies of files such as programs or documents. It only requires a diff file be kept as each new version of a file is created. This will generally be many times smaller than keeping the total file each time.

7.2.4. Differences between 3 versions of a file

Command:	diff3
Syntax:	diff3 [-ex3] file1 file2 file3
Function:	This command allows you to compare three different versions of a file and find out what the differences are. The basic information provided after a run is:

- All three files are different
- file1 is different
- file2 is different
- file3 is different

The information given is suficient to reconstruct an earlier file to look like the latest one.

Option:	There are three options available. They are:
-e	produces output in a format acceptable to the ed editor.
-x3	produces output that will allow the incorporation of only changes different in file3.

Example:

(1) The first example is to show the command usage without any options. The three files are:

```
file1              file2              file3
1 line one         1 line one         1 line one
3 line three       3 line three       3 line three
7 line seven       6 line six         7 line seven
6 line six         2 line two         6 line six
2 line two         7 line seven       5 line five
5 line five        5 line five        2 line two
4 line four        4 line four        4 line four
```

The command is:

```
user   ->    diff3 file1 file2 file3 <r>
UNIX   ->    ====2
       ->    1:2a
       ->    2:3,4c
       ->    6 line six
       ->    2 line two
       ->    3:2a
       ->    ====
       ->    1:4,5c
       ->    6 line six
       ->    2 line two
       ->    2:5a
       ->    3:4c
       ->    6 line six
       ->    ====3
       ->    1:6a
       ->    2:6a
       ->    3:6c
       ->    2 line two
       ->    $
```

The preceding information provided us with the the differences in each of the files. The format is:

(1) file: line number append

the first entry "1:2a" would translate to

file 1: line 2 append

which is saying that something must be appended after line 2 of file1 in order to bring it in line with file 2.

(2)   file: line number , line number change

The second entry   "2:3,4c "
                    " 6 line six "
                    " 2 line two " would translate to

ctrlinefile 2: line 3 to line 4 change

which is saying that lines 3 and 4 must change in file 2 to bring it in line. These two formats describe the differences between the three files along with "====" telling you which file is different.

(3)   The next example uses the same data files, but will use the option -e to produce code acceptable to the ed editor.

```
user   ->    diff3 -e file1 file2 file3 <r>
UNIX   ->    6a
       ->    2 line two
       ->    .
       ->    4,5c
       ->    6 line six
       ->    .
       ->    $
```

In this example we are shown the changes (in ed format) that are necessary to incorporate into file 1 all the changes between files 2 and 3. If we wanted only the changes flagged in file 3 and not file 2, we could run with the option "-x(-3)".

Summary:

This command is generally used with three versions of the same file. It provides you with the means by which to keep backup copies three deep and still be able to create one copy from the others.

7.2.5. Find Pattern Matches in Files

Command:	grep
Syntax:	grep [option]... expression [file]
Function:	This command is used when a string pattern is to be located in one or more files. In the case of a single file one could simply edit the file and search for the pattern desired. However grep is useful when more than one file is involved. The single command "grep" can locate all occurences of a pattern without having to look at each individual file. Grep patterns are limited regular expressions similar to those used in the ed editor.
Option:	The following options can be used:

-v   All lines but those matching are printed.
-c   Only a count of matching lines is printed.
-l   The names of files with matching lines are listed(once) separated by newlines.
-n   Each line is preceded by its line number in the file.
-b   Each line is preceded by the block number on which it was found.
-s   No output is produced, only status.
-h   Do not print filename headers with output lines.
-y   Lower case letters in the pattern will also match upper case letters in the input.
-e   expression
     Used when a pattern starts with "-".

Example:

(1) In our previous command descriptions, we used several files that were similar. They were files "file1,file2, file3". They are:

file1	file2	file3
1 line one	1 line one	1 line one
3 line three	3 line three	3 line three
7 line seven	6 line six	7 line seven
6 line six	2 line two	6 line six
2 line two	7 line seven	5 line five
5 line five	5 line five	2 line two
4 line four	4 line four	4 line four

To find all of the occurrences of "seven" we can say:

```
user   ->   grep seven file1 file2 file3 <r>
UNIX   ->   file1:7 line seven
       ->   file2:7 line seven
       ->   file3:7 line seven
       ->   $
```

The information obtained provides us with the file name and a listing of the complete line. We could have written this command two different ways and still obtained the same information.

(1) grep seven file? <r>

(2) grep seven fil* <r>

In both cases we must be sure that those are the only files with that file name pattern(i.e., file names: file5 or filtemp).

(2) In the previous example we found that the lines containing the patterns were located, but not where they were in each of the files. We can use the -n option to obtain the line number for each occurrence. Thus we can say:

```
user   ->   grep -n seven file? <r>
UNIX   ->   file1:3:7 line seven
       ->   file2:5:7 line seven
```

```
->    file3:3:7 line seven
->    $
```

The only difference between this example and the previous one is that the line numbers have been included. The entry reads (from left to right) file name, line number, line.

(3) Another case is where we are looking for a pattern that could exist in upper or lower case letters. Because of the large number of combinations it would be too dificult to search on all possible patterns. Thus the option -y provides us with a single way to express it. For this example we have edited a file to contain some upper case letters. The file looks as follows:

```
filex
1 line one
3 line three
7 line seven
6 line six
2 line Two
5 line Five
4 line Four
```

We can then enter the command:

```
user   ->   grep -y f filex <r>
UNIX  ->    5 line Five
      ->    4 line Four
      ->    $
```

In this case we were looking for anything that contained an "f or F".

(4) We can also combine options to give us additional information when necessary. In the previous case we could look for upper case letters only. If we wanted the line numbers as well (option -n) we could say:

```
user   ->   grep -y -n f filex <r>
```

```
UNIX  ->    6:5 line Five
      ->    7:4 line Four
      ->    $
```

Notice that in the previous two examples the file name is not given. This happens when only one file is named. The last example provided us with the line numbers as well as the lines themselves.

Summary:

Grep can be very useful when a large number of files are involved. An example of how it's used can be seen in locating a pattern(say a variable name) in several c programs enabling you to change or delete them.

7.2.6. Octal Dump

Command:	od
Syntax:	od [-bcdox] file [[+]offset[.][b]]
Function:	The octal dump program provides the facility to dump a file or part of a file in one or more formats as specified by the options. For example, it is useful in determining if there are some hidden characters in the text that are causing problems.
Option:	Several options exist that provide the capability to see the text in different formats. These options are:
b	Each byte is interpreted in octal.
c	Each byte is interpreted in ASCII, with the hidden characters being displayed in a special format. These formats are:

1) null = \0
2) backspace = \b
3) formfeed = \f
4) newline = \n
5) return = \r
6) tab = \t
7) Others = 3 digit octal numbers

d   Each word is interpreted in decimal.
o   Each word is interpreted in octal(default).
x   Each word is interpreted in hex.

Example:

(1) Let's first look at a simple octal dump of a two line file. The content
     of the file is:

     filea
     1 1 2 1 1
     2 2 1 2 2

user   ->   **od filea <r>**
UNIX ->

     0000000 030440 030440 031040 030440
     0000000 030412 031040 031040 030440
     0000020 031040 031012
     0000024

           ->   **$**

This is just a plan octal dump of the two line file "filea".

(2) This next example will show the same octal dump; however, it will use
     the option -b which dumps the data one line at a time.

user   ->   od -b filea <r>
UNIX ->

      0000000 061 040 061 040 062 040 061 040
      0000000 061 012 062 040 062 040 061 040
      0000020 062 040 062 012
      0000024

          -> $

      This is exactly the same output as the previous example with the ex-
ception that it is represented one character at a time instead of one word
at a time.

(3) The most useful option is the one that presents the text in ASCII,
     but displays all the hidden characters. There are many times when
     something doesn't work properly and it is because there exists one or
     more of these hidden characters.

user   ->   od -c filea <r>
UNIX ->

      0000000 1 1 2 1 1 \n 2 2 1
      0000020 2 2 \n
      0000024

          -> $

In this example the only hidden characters are the newline characters "\n". However, if they were not supposed to be there, they would not be visible without the use of this command.

Summary: The principal use of this command is during debug, whether it be a computer program or a document being formatted.

7.2.7. Table of Contents For Archive Files

Command: ranlib

Syntax: ranlib archive file

Function: This command is useful when dealing with archive files that contain program object modules used by the loader. It produces a table of contents at the beginning of an archive file that allows the loader to find all references to all object programs in the file during a single pass. Without this table of contents it would be required to arrange the object programs such that a single pass could be made over the archive file in order to find all the references.

Option: No options exist for this command.

Example:

(1) There is nothing to do but enter the command name and the name of the archive file. The table of contents will be generated. It should be noted however that once this table of contents exists, any changes will make the table of contents invalid until it is run again. If you forget to run it after a change, and then use it it will tell you it's out of date.

```
user   ->   ranlib library <r>
```

UNIX -> $

No message will be produced unless there is a problem. The table of contents named "_.SYMDEF" will be produced and placed at the beginning of the archive file.

Summary:

This command is useful only when used in conjunction with the loader. It eliminates the need to organize the programs within the archive file.

7.2.8. Word Count

Command:	wc
Syntax:	wc [-lwc] [file. . .]
Function:	This command provides a count of the number of lines, number of words, and number of characters of one or more files. A line is delimited by a newline character "\n", a word is delimited by spaces, tabs or newline, and a character is just that: every character in the file.
Option:	The options allow the user to specify only those statistics (s)he requires. They are:

l	count the number of lines in the file.
w	count the number of words in the file.
c	count the number of characters in the file.

Example:

(1) First let's use the basic command with a simple file. The contents of the file are:

```
file1
1 line one
3 line three
7 line seven
6 line six
2 line two
5 line five
4 line four


        ->    $
```

We can then execute the command:

```
user    ->   wc file1 <r>
UNIX  ->   7    21    83 file1
        ->    $
```

To read this we find first the number of lines which is 7, and then the number of words which is 21, and finally the number of characters 83 followed by the file name.

(2) We can use the options to obtain only that data we need. For example, if we only need the number of lines in the file we can say:

```
user    ->   wc -l file1 <r>
UNIX  ->   7 file1
        ->    $
```

This gives us only the number of lines and the file name.

(3) Another way of using this command is to get the count of a large number of files. For example, you may want to know how many lines and characters there are in a group of programs that are used as a single

system. Let's say that the files that start with "fil" are the programs that make up this set. To see the total count on lines and characters we need only say:

```
user    ->   wc -lc fil* <r>
UNIX  ->   7    83 file1
      ->   7    83 file1.c
      ->   1    5 file1.o
      ->   7    83 file2
      ->   7    83 file3
      ->   0    83 filen
      ->   29   420 total
      ->   $
```

Reading from left to right, we have the number of lines, followed by the number of characters and the name of the file. The last line contains the total count for both the lines and the characters.

Summary:

This command can be used anytime you need to know the count for lines, words, and characters in a file or files.

7.2.9. Report Repeated Lines in a File

Command: uniq

Syntax: uniq [-options [+n] [-n]] [input] [output]

Function: This command looks for adjacent lines that are the same. In the default case (no options) all but the first line of those that are the same are deleted. Thus if 4 consecutive lines are the same, then the lines 2, 3, and 4 are deleted. The output file will consist of lines that are different.

Option:	Three options exist which perform the following functions:
u	Only the lines that are not repeated are output.
d	Only the repeated lines are output.
c	generate an output(as with no option) with the number of occurrences of each line appearing at the beginning of the line.

The arguments (+n and -n) specify skipping an initial portion of each line in the comparison.

+n	The first n fields together with any blanks before each are ignored. A field is defined as a string of non-space, non-tab characters separated by tabs and spaces from its neighbors.
-n	The first n characters are ignored. Fields are skipped before characters.

Example:

(1) Let's start with a simple file as follows and generate a new file eliminating all second and succeeding copies of repeated lines.

The file "f1" is:

```
1 line one
3 line three
3 line three
7 line seven
6 line six
2 line two
2 line two
5 line five
4 line four
```

```
user     ->     uniq f1 f2<r>
UNIX     ->     $
user     ->     cat f2<r>
UNIX     ->     1 line one
         ->     3 line three
         ->     7 line seven
         ->     6 line six
         ->     2 line two
         ->     5 line five
         ->     4 line four
         ->     $
```

We can see that the new file "f2" contains only lines that are not repeated. If more than two occurrences of a line exist it is treated the same way, that is to say, all but the first occurrence is deleted. We should also notice that the file must be in order(see sort) or we will not find other occurrences.

(2) This example will use the option -u to output only the lines that are not repeated.

```
user     ->     uniq -u f1<r>       direct output to terminal
UNIX     ->     1 line one
         ->     7 line seven
         ->     6 line six
         ->     5 line five
         ->     4 line four
         ->     $
```

The two lines 2 and 3 which were repeated are not output at all.

(3) There may be times when all we want are the lines that are repeated. In this case we can use the option -d.

```
user     ->     uniq -d f1<r>
```

```
UNIX  ->    3 line three
      ->    2 line two
      ->    $
```

(4) Now let's get the count of the number of occurrences of each line. This
     is done using the option -c.

```
user   ->    uniq -c f1<r>
UNIX   ->    1 1 line one
       ->    2 3 line three
       ->    1 7 line seven
       ->    1 6 line six
       ->    2 2 line two
       ->    1 5 line five
       ->    1 4 line four
       ->    $
```

The first number is the number of occurrences of that line. Thus line
2 and 5 have two occurrences while the rest all have only one occurrence.

(5) There will be a time when you will want to make your selection based
     only on part of the line. In this case the arguments +n and -n are
     available so that you can skip an initial portion of each line. The op-
     tions allow you to skip a number of fields and/or a number of charac-
     ters. Lets' use a file that contains matching data in the first field. This
     file "f3" looks as follows.

```
file "f3"
1 line one
3 line three
3 line three3
7 line seven
6 line six
2 line two
2 line two2
5 line five
4 line four
```

```
user   ->   uniq -1 f3<r>
UNIX   ->   1 line one
       ->   3 line three
       ->   3 line three3
       ->   7 line seven
       ->   6 line six
       ->   2 line two
       ->   2 line two2
       ->   5 line five
       ->   4 line four
       ->   $
```

As we can see, the only difference occurred in the first field and we skipped it, thus we were able to output all the lines. If the option had not been used, lines 3 and 7 would have been deleted from the output.

Summary:

Remember that the repeated lines must be in adjacent order to be found. This can be accomplished by using the sort command. In the examples we did not specify an output file so that the output would be directed to the terminal. Normally you would specify an output file.

7.2.10. Split a File Into Pieces

Command: split

Syntax: split [-n] [file [name]]

Function: This command splits a file into n-line pieces (default 1000 lines), as many as are necessary onto a set of output files. If a name is given for the output file, the letters aa,ab,ac,... will be appended to the end of the output file for each file that is generated. If no output file is given then the name "x" is provided.

Option: Only one option exists for this command. It is -n
                        and specifies the number of lines the command is
                        to place in each output file.

Example:

(1) Let's use the file "f1" from the example in section 7.2.9 (command
     uniq). We will then split this file into two (2) line files starting with
     the name "ff".

```
user   ->    split -2 f1 ff<r>
UNIX   ->    $
user   ->    ls *<r>
UNIX   ->    f1
       ->    ffaa
       ->    ffab
       ->    ffac
       ->    ffad
       ->    ffae
       ->    $
```

```
user   ->    cat ffaa ffab ffac ffad ffae<r>
UNIX   ->    1 line one
       ->    3 line three
       ->    3 line three
       ->    7 line seven
       ->    6 line six
       ->    2 line two
       ->    2 line two
       ->    5 line five
       ->    4 line four
       ->    $
```

If we were to list the file "f1", we would see the same thing. The only
difference is that the lines are now contained in five (5) different files.

Summary:

The main use for this command is to split your data into smaller files when (1) they become too large to manage, or (2) when they exceed the limits of a file used by various programs such as the editor "ed".

7.2.11. Sort or Merge Files

Command:	sort
Syntax:	sort [-option. . .] [+pos1 [-pos2]]. . . [-o name] [-T directory] [name]. . .
Function:	This command sorts or merges files together and writes the result on the spcified file (default is standard output). If no sort key is specified, the default is the complete line. A file can be sorted based on one or more keys and in order as specified by the options.
Option:	The following options are available with this command:
b	this option causes the sort to ignore leading blanks(spaces and tabs) in the field comparisons.
c	Check that the input file is sorted according to the ordering rules; no output is provided unless the file is out of sort.
d	"dictionary" order: only letters,digits and blanks are significant in comparisons.
f	treat upper case letters as if they are lower case letters.
i	ignore characters outside the ASCII range 040-0176 in nonnumeric comparisons.

m	this option specifies that the named files are to be merged. It expects the input files to have already been sorted.
n	sorted by arithmetic value. A numeric string can consist of optional blanks, optional minus sign, and zero or more digits with optional decimal point.
o	the name following this option specifies a file where the output is to be placed. If it doesn't exist, then the output goes to the standard output.
r	reverse the sense of comparisons (i.e., numeric values would be ordered starting with the largest value down to the lowest value).
tx	the "t" specifies that a tab character other than the default (blanks) is to be used as the separator. The x is the actual character to be used as the separator.
T	this option allows you to name a directory where all the temporary files used by the command will be held.
u	when two or more lines match the same key, only one of them is output. This is to eliminate duplicates,etc.

Specifying keys on which to sort is accomplished by use of the arguments (+pos1 and -pos2). Each of these pairs can be used to restrict a sort key to a field beginning at pos1 and ending at pos2. Pos1 tells the sort to skip a number of fields starting from the beginning of the line. Pos2 tells the sort to skip a number of characters into the field specified by pos1.

Example:

(1) Let's first sort a file on each complete line. In other words the sort key is the complete line. This is the default when no options are specified.

The file "file1" is to be sorted.

    1 line one
    3 line three
    7 line seven

```
6 line six
2 line two
5 line five
4 line four
```

```
user    ->    sort file1<r>
UNIX    ->    1 line one
        ->    2 line two
        ->    3 line three
        ->    4 line four
        ->    5 line five
        ->    6 line six
        ->    7 line seven
        ->    $
```

(2) We can just as easily sort the same file in reverse order by using the option "-r".

```
user    ->    sort -r file1<r>
UNIX    ->    7 line seven
        ->    6 line six
        ->    5 line five
        ->    4 line four
        ->    3 line three
        ->    2 line two
        ->    1 line one
        ->    $
```

In each of these two cases the sort key was the entire line. If we had wanted to sort only on the numeric value in the first field, we could have the option "-n". If the field is the first in the line, the position arguments (pos) need not be used. However if the field is anywhere else in the line, it will have to be used. Let's look at an example using these options.

(3) First sort on the first field which is numeric.

```
user   ->    sort -n file1 -o outfile<r>
UNIX  ->    $
```

The file will look exactly like the sorted file from example 1. But in this case we requested that the results be placed in the file "outfile".

(4) We could also sort using the number option if the sort key were other than the first field by using the "pos" arguments. Let's say that the number field is the last instead of the first field in the line. We would then say:

```
user   ->    sort -n +2 file2 -o outfile<r>
UNIX  ->    $
```

The results are placed in the output file named "outfile". The sort key used is the third field even though we have used the argument +2. This is because the first field is zero, the second one, the third two and so on.

(5) We can also use multiple options together where they do not conflict. For example we can sort on a numeric field and request that the output be reversed.

```
user   ->    sort -nr file1 -o file2<r>
UNIX  ->    $
```

The output has been sorted on the first field which is numeric and output with the largest value being first and the lowest value being last.

Summary:

The sort command is a very powerful function and will be useful in solving many problems. The examples we have shown are only a few of the ways in which it can be used. The best way to learn is to use these examples as a basis and try other options.

7.2.12. Questions

(1) You have a tape containing EBCDIC characters and you want to read it into your computer (tape drive = mt0). What command is used and what are the parameters?

(2) What command (and parameters) would you use to generate a set of difference commmands compatible with the ed editor (use file1 and file2 as two of the parameters)?

(3) You have six files in a directory each containing text. What command can be issued to locate all occurrences of the pattern "syntax"?

(4) What do the following commands do?

a) wc file1

b) split -10 file1 F

c) sort -r file1 -o file2

7.3. Running of Programs

This set of commands lends itself to the execution of programs. They are especially useful during the execution of shell files (see chapter 6). They cover such things as setting up the automatic executing of programs at some specific time,or spooling a process and waiting for it to finish, etc.

7.3.1. Echo Arguments

Command:	echo
Syntax:	echo [-n] [arg]. . .
Function:	This command writes its arguments separated by blanks and terminated by a newline on the standard output. This is especially useful when using shell files and you want to know what is happening as it happens.
Option:	The only option "-n" is to provide a facility to eliminate the newline which is added to the end of each argument. In this case the arguments will appear one after another separated by a blank.

Example:

(1) Create a shell file that executes several commands and echoes the start of each command.

We will first create our shell file "echo" as:

```
echo starting command 1
command 1
echo starting command 2
command 2
echo starting command 3
command 3
echo end of shell file
```

We can then execute the shell file as defined in chapter 6.

```
user    ->    sh echo<r>
```

```
UNIX  ->    starting command 1
      ->    starting command 2
      ->    starting command 3
      ->    end of shell file
      ->    $
```

This command is useful when you want an audit trail of what is happening during the execution of a shell file. Another use is when you want to see if the shell file is executing correctly.

(2) We can also echo the names of arguments that are passed to a shell file. This can be useful when we want to know that the right argument is passed at the right time, or just to create an audit trail. The shell file "echo1" is:

```
echo $1
command 1 $1
echo $2
command 2 $2
echo end of shell file
```

We can then envoke it by:

```
user  ->    sh echo1 test1 test2<r>
UNIX  ->    test1
      ->    test2
      ->    end of shell file
      ->    $
```

As we can see by this example, all we are doing is printing the arguments that were being passed to a shell file. This may appear to be of no value, but there will be many cases when you will be calling a shell file from another shell file and the arguments are not coming directly from you.

Summary:

The echo command is used in many ways, some of which have been shown here. One that hasn't is issuing instructions when some interaction

is required between the user and the programs. You will find other uses as
you become more familiar with it.

7.3.2. Terminate a Process With Extreme Prejudice

Command: kill

Syntax: kill [-option] processid. . .

Function: This command is used to kill a process when it is
                    tying up the system or you have decided that it is
                    not needed just after you invoked it. The process
                    ID can be obtained by use of the command "ps".
                    The processes specified to be killed must belong to
                    you unless you are the superuser.

Option: The only option allowed with this command is a
                    signal number. This will kill processes that do not
                    catch the default signal. For example the option
                    "-9" is a sure kill. You can shut the system down
                    with a kill "-1 1".

Example:

(1) Let's say that you start a spooled print. Because the spooler starts
    the job and returns control to you, you will have to find the process
    number before you can kill it (terminate it). First you must issue a
    "ps" command to find the process id. Once you have it, you can then
    issue the kill command along with the process id.

```
user   ->   ps<r>
UNIX  ->
```

PID   TTY   TIME   CMD

```
1455    co     0:01
3130    2      0:03
4317    2      0:41
4354    ?      <defunct>
4355    2      0:00
4356    2      0:03           lpr


$
```

In this case you have only requested your own active processes. Because you are terminal (tty) 2, you can look at the functions being performed. From this you select the one that you want to terminate and issue the kill command. Because the one you want to terminate is the line spooler, you can see that the process id is "4356".

```
user    ->    kill 4356<r>
UNIX    ->    $
```

Just to be sure that the correct process was killed, you can issue another "ps". The process "4356" should be terminated (not there).

```
user    ->    ps<r>
UNIX    ->
```

```
PID    TTY    TIME           CMD
1455    co     0:01
3130    2      0:03
4317    2      0:41
4354    ?      <defunct>
4355    2      0:00


$
```

Summary:

This command should be used carefully, because if you kill the wrong process, you may terminate yourself and the system will log you out. It is probably a good idea to use the option "-9" to insure that you have killed the process.

7.3.3. Suspend Execution for an Interval

Command:	sleep
Syntax:	sleep time
Function:	This command allows you to suspend execution for some designated period of time (where "time" is in seconds). This provides you with the ability to delay the execution of a command perhaps until something else completes.
Option:	There are no options for this command.

Example:

(1) Let's say that we want to remind someone else on the system that they will have to perform some designated task one hour from now. If we are not going to be around, we can say:

```
user    ->    sleep 3600<r>
        ->    write sam<r>
        ->    Please perform the designated task
        ->                          cnt'l-d
```

The system will wait for 3600 seconds before issuing the message. The problem here is that we cannot logoff the system. In the next chapter we will learn how to create shell procedures that can be invoked at a later time, but for now all we want to show is how the sleep command might be used.

Summary:

There exist many reasons for using this command. The knowledge that it exists will allow you to use it as you find the need.

7.3.4. Run a Command at Low Priority

Command:	nice
Syntax:	nice [-number] command [arguments]
Function:	This command allows you to execute a command with a low scheduling priority, i.e., you can execute it without having much effect on other commands you are executing. If the "-number" is provided, it causes the priority to be incremented. The higher the number, the lower the priority. This is valid up to a limit of 20, with 10 being the default if no number is provided.
Option:	No options exist for this command.

Example:

(1) Let's dump a directory of files while we are using the editor.

```
user   ->   nice -20 tar c0 working&<r>
UNIX   ->   234                 process number
       ->   $
user   ->   ed file1<r>
       ->   .
```

```
->  .
->  .
```

As we can see, the only difference will be that the tar dump executes at a low priority providing us with more cpu time to edit our program "file1".

Summary:

As with the sleep command there will be times when this command is of value. It is probably used most frequently by the system administrator when performing tasks during normal or heavy use of the system.

7.3.5. Pipe Fitting

Command:	tee
Syntax:	tee [options] [file]. . .
Function:	This command provides you with the capability to echo something to your terminal (standard output) and at the same time save it in a file. This is more frequently used when you are executing a shell procedure (see chapter 8).
Option:	Two options exist for this command. They are:
-i	• ignores interrupts
-a	• causes the output to be appended to the files rather than overwriting them.

Example:

(1) We have a series of commands to execute and want to keep a record of the order in which they were executed.

The series of commands could appear as:

tee command1 -a file1

command1

tee command2 -a file1

command2

tee command3 -a file1

command3

If executed, the results would appear as:

```
UNIX  ->    command1
      ->    command2
      ->    command3
      ->    $
user  ->    cat file1<r>
UNIX  ->    command1
      ->    command2
      ->    command3
      ->    $
```

We can see from this example that the data saved in the file is the same as what is echoed to the terminal. This is useful when you are running a set of commands and cannot watch them complete, but need to know if they executed properly.

Summary:

The use of this command can be better understood after reading chapter 8 on the use of shell files.

7.3.6. Questions

(1) What is the purpose of the echo command?

(2) You have created a process that is not needed. The process number is 102. What is the command used to terminate this process? How can you check to be sure that it was terminated?

(3) Provide the command that will cause a long running program to execute with minimum impact on any other programs currently running.

7.4. Status Inquiries

There will be times when you will need information about the system or just information in general. The availability of commands that are easy to use, and provide you with information on the system such as file and directory information, free space on a file system, amount of space you have used in a directory, who's on the system, etc., are very valuable. In addition you can obtain information about the date, time, etc.

These commands provide you with this type of information any time you find that you need it. The following commands are available:

7.4.1. List the Contents of a Directory

Command:	ls
Syntax:	ls [-options. . .] name. . .
Function:	This command provides you with information about your directories and files such as read/write permissions, date of last change, etc. The standard output using only the "ls" command without options provides you with a sorted output (alphabetically) of the names of all files and directories under the directory you are currently positioned at.
Option:	There are several options that can prove to be useful in selecting and ordering your list. These are:
l	Provides a list in long form (see chapter 4).

t	•sort by time modified (latest first) instead of by name as is normal.
a	•list all entries. Usually "." entries are not listed.
s	•give the size in blocks, including indirect blocks, for each entry.
d	•give the status information of the named directory (-l option data) and don't provide its contents (files and directories under it).
r	•reverse the order of the sort to get the names of the files and directories in reverse alpha- betic order.
u	•this uses time of last access instead of last modification for sorting
c	•use the time of last modification to inode (mode, etc.) instead of last modification to file for sort-ing.
i	•print i-number in first column of the report for each file listed.
f	•force each argument to be interpreted as a direc-tory and list the name found in each slot. This option turns off -l, -t, -s, and -r and turns on -a. The order is the order in which entries appear in the directory.
g	•provide the group ID instead of owner ID in long listing.

Example:

(1) We have already seen the basic use of the "ls" command in chapter 4. Here we will look at a few of the options that may be useful. The first of these options is the use of "-a" which provides the user with the ability to see all entries because the system usually suppresses entries starting with "." and "..".

```
user   ->   ls -al<r>
UNIX  ->

total 829
```

```
drwxrwxr-x 4     dick     1376     Jan 12 10:30    .
drwxrwxr-x 13    dick     400      Jan 17 10:49    ..
-rw-rw-r- 1      dick     5705     Dec 21 15:35    ar
drwxrwxr-x 2     dick     704      Dec 20 13:48    book
-rw-rw-r- 1      dick     3207     Dec 22 08:55    cat
-rw-rw-r- 1      dick     18371    Jan 2 18:47     ch5
-rw-rw-r- 1      dick     1009     Jan 5 15:31     ch7.accn
-rw-rw-r- 1      dick     1466     Jan 5 15:34     ch7.bkup
-rw-rw-r- 1      dick     23807    Jan 5 15:38     ch7.inf
-rw-rw-r- 1      dick     627      Jan 3 18:30     ch7.stat
-rw-rw-r- 1      dick     9756     Jan 5 14:05     chapt2
-rw-rw-r- 1      dick     21570    Jan 5 14:41     chapt4
-rw-rw-r- 1      dick     36678    Jan 6 20:39     chapt5
-rw-rw-r- 1      dick     10362    Jan 5 15:28     chapt6
-rw-rw-r- 1      dick     597      Dec 23 15:16    df
-rw-rw-r- 1      dick     2915     Dec 21 21:14    diff
```

UNIX ->   **$**

The only difference between this ls command and one not using the "-a" option is that the first two entries would not have been displayed. Notice that if the "l" option had not been used, the output would have been only the names. Thus multiple options can be used with caution in a single " ls" command.

(2) Now let's look at the same list, but sorted according to the time each entry was modified. This is listed as latest modified first instead of by name.

```
user    ->    ls -tl<r>
UNIX  ->
```

```
total 829
-rw-rw-r- 1 dick        36678    Jan 6 20:39     chapt5
```

-rw-rw-r- 1	dick	23807	Jan 5 15:38	ch7.inf
-rw-rw-r- 1	dick	1466	Jan 5 15:34	ch7.bkup
-rw-rw-r- 1	dick	1009	Jan 5 15:31	ch7.accn
-rw-rw-r- 1	dick	10362	Jan 5 15:28	chapt6
-rw-rw-r- 1	dick	21570	Jan 5 14:41	chapt4
-rw-rw-r- 1	dick	9756	Jan 5 14:05	chapt2
-rw-rw-r- 1	dick	627	Jan 3 18:30	ch7.stat
-rw-rw-r- 1	dick	18371	Jan 2 18:47	ch5
-rw-rw-r- 1	dick	597	Dec 23 15:16	df
-rw-rw-r- 1	dick	3207	Dec 22 08:55	cat
-rw-rw-r- 1	dick	2915	Dec 21 21:14	diff
-rw-rw-r- 1	dick	5705	Dec 21 15:35	ar
drwxrwxr-x 2	dick	704	Dec 20 13:48	book

UNIX -> $

We can see from this example that although the same information is provided, it is in a totally different format. This command is useful when you are trying to find out what files have been most recently modified. We can use more than one option at a time; however, you should be sure that they do not conflict with each other. For example you would not want to use the options "t and u" together, because they both order the output in a different way.

Summary:

This command is described in chapter 4 using only the "-l" option. However there will be times when you will find other options a great benefit to you in obtaining additional information.

7.4.2. Print and Set Date

Command: date

Syntax: date [yymmddhhmm[.ss]]

Function: This command is used by most users to get the date and time. However the system administrator must have the ability to set the date and time whenever starting or restarting the system.

Option: The options consist of:

yy   year (if year doesn't change, not needed)
mm   month (value 01 to 12)
dd   day (value 01 to 31) depends on month
hh   hour of the day (24 hour clock)
mm   minutes (00 to 60)
.ss   seconds (00 to 60)

Example:

(1) Any time the user wants to know the time and/or date, this command can be executed.

```
user  ->   date<r>
UNIX  ->   Sat Jan 10 14:51:02 EST 1981
      ->   $
```

This command can be issued at any time by any user.

(2) The setting or resetting of the date is generally done by the systems administrator. However anyone who has permission can set or reset the date and time.

```
user  ->   date 8101101816<r>
UNIX  ->   Sat Jan 10 18:16 EST 1981
      ->   $
```

Summary:

This command is just another of the useful commands found in UNIX. Although it may not be used frequently, when it is, it is very useful. How many times have you been caught without your watch and needed to know the time and/or date?

7.4.3. Who is On the System

Command: who

Syntax: who [who-file] [am I]

Function: This command provides a list of all the users currently on the system and what terminal they are connected to.

Option: Two options exist for this command. The first is a file that provides the "who" command with the necessary information that is normally (default) provided by the system file "/etc/utmp". Typically the given file will be /usr/adm/wtmp, which contains a record of all the logins since it was created. The second option "am I" tells you who you are logged in as.

Example:

(1) Let's first try this command without any options.

```
user   ->   who<r>
UNIX  ->   darrin ttyb Jan 11 08:32
      ->   dick ttya Jan 11 09:44
      ->   pat ttyh Jan 11 14:12
      ->   $
```

The information provided includes the user's name, terminal, date and time of login.

(2) Next let's see what the command does when the option "am I" is used.

```
user  ->   who am i<r>
UNIX  ->   dick tty1 Jan 17 11:22
      ->   $
```

Summary:

This command is useful when you want to write to someone else and you want to see if they are logged in, or maybe you need their correct login name. There will also be times when you need to know the terminal you or others are using.

7.4.4. Get Terminal Name

Command: tty

Syntax: tty

Function: This command prints the terminal name that you are currently using.

Option: No options exist for this command.

Example:

(1) Since there is only one use of this command, it produces the following output.

```
user   ->   tty<r>
```

```
UNIX  ->   ttyx
      ->   $
```

Summary:

Although you can obtain the same information by using the command "who am i", it is just a simple way of getting this information.

7.4.5. Working Directory Name

Command:	pwd
Syntax:	pwd
Function:	This command provides you with a complete pathname to your current (working) directory.
Option:	No options exist for this command.

Example:

(1) There exists only one form of usage for this commmand.

```
user  ->   pwd
UNIX  ->   /rlg/dick/book
```

Summary:

This command is very useful when you are not sure where you are. This command is explained in more detail in chapter 4.

7.4.6. Process Status

Command:	ps
Syntax:	ps [option. . .] [namelist]
Function:	This command provides you with information about what is currently active in the system. Depending on the options used, this command will provide you with information about all the processes with or without terminals, long listings or short listings.
Option:	Three (3) options exist for this command. They can be used separately or together.
a	• this option asks for information about all the processes associated with all terminals. In other words, all the processes that have been invoked from a terminal.
x	• this option asks for information about all the processes that are not associated with a terminal. These are generally processes invoked by the system.
l	• This option provides you with a long listing. This listing displays many things about the current status of the system. See examples for more detailed information.

Example:

(1) First let's try it with no options.

user   ->   ps<r>

```
UNIX  ->


PID    TTY    TIME            CMD
203    co     0:03
741    co     0:35
751    ?      <defunct>
752    co     0:00            te status
753    co     0:03



$        ->
```

As we can see from this example we are provided with information about our status. The information provided is:

    o process ID
    o terminal number for controlling tty
    o cumulative execution time for the process
    o process command (what it's doing)

The process ID is necessary when you have done something wrong and have to kill that process (see kill command). The process description tries to tell you what you are doing in that process. For example, the first process says you are in the shell. This is almost always the case because anytime you are logged into the system you are placed under control of the shell. The next process says that the program "te status" is being executed. This happens to be a program that is being executed with one argument which is "status". The next two processes define the execution of the "ps" command itself. This is because I executed it directly from the editor.

(2) Now let's execute the ps command with the option "a" to obtain the status on all users.

```
user   ->   ps a<r>
UNIX  ->
```

PID	TTY	TIME	CMD
1494	co	0:01	
27	1	0:00	- x
15	?	1:07	
21	lp	0:00	
28	2	0:00	- 0
1553	5	0:00	
30	6	0:00	- x
852	7	0:08	
1700	co	0:01	
1706	co	0:22	
1713	?	<defunct>	
1714	co	0:00	
1715	co	0:04	.sp

This option simply provides the same information as was shown for an individual user, but in this case for all active users on the system, whereas the previous example displayed only the requesting user's information.

(3) Now we will look at all the processes being used instead of only our own, but including more detail.

```
user   ->   ps axl<r>
UNIX   ->
```

F	S	UID	PID	PPID	CPU	PRI	NICE	ADDR	SZ	WCHAN	TTY	TIME	CMD
3	S	0	0	0	147	0	20	57	4	7670	?	1196:56	swapper
1	S	0	1	0	0	30	20	377	12	10574	?	0:02	
1	S	4	1494	1	0	30	20	323	16	10630	co	0:01	
1	S	0	27	1	0	28	20	365	12	107574	1	0:00	- x
1	S	0	13	1	0	40	20	351	12	164000	?	1:10	
1	S	1	15	1	0	40	20	332	28	164000	?	1:07	
1	S	0	21	1	0	29	20	341	12	110264	1p	0:00	
1	S	0	28	1	0	28	20	362	12	110104	2	0:00	- 0
1	S	0	1553	1	0	28	20	173	12	110022	5	0:00	
1	S	0	30	1	0	28	20	354	12	110166	6	0:00	- x
1	S	6	852	1	0	28	20	262	16	110332	7	0:08	
1	S	0	1700	1494	0	30	20	127	16	11224	co	0:01	
1	S	0	1706	1700	4	26	20	74	40	56356	co	0:32	
1	Z	0	1719	1706	5	50	20	0	0		?		<defunct>
1	S	0	1720	1706	0	30	20	123	16	11350	co	0:00	
1	R	0	1721	1720	173	60	20	214	24		co	0:05	.sp

As we can see this option provides us with a lot more information than any of the previous. From left to right, the information shown consists of:

F	flags associated with the process (01: in core, 02: system process, 04: locked in core (physical I/O), 10: being swapped, 20: being traced by another process)).
S	the state of the process (0: nonexistent, S: sleeping, W: waiting, R: running, I: intermediate, Z: terminated, T: stopped).
UID	the user ID of the process owner
PID	the process ID of the process (used with the kill command)
PPID	the process ID of the parent process
CPU	processor utilization for scheduling
PRI	the priority of the process; high numbers mean low priority
NICE	used in priority computation
ADDR	the core address of the process if resident, otherwise the disk address
SZ	the size i blocks of the core image of the process
WCHAN	the event for which the process is waiting or sleeping; if blank, the process is running

TTY   the controlling tty for the process
TIME   the cumulative execution time for the process

Summary:

This command is generally used by the system administrator when there are problems with the system such as process table overflow, program out of control, etc. However sometimes a user may have started a job and then decided that it should be terminated. This can be accomplished by using the ps command, obtaining the PID and killing the process associated with that program. For more information see chapter 9.

7.4.7. Summarize Disk Usage

Command: du

Syntax: du [-s] [-a] [name. . .]

Function: This command provides you with the number of blocks used by each file and a total count for all files. The command will obtain this information for all files in the current directory and all its sub-directories.

Option: Two options exist for this command. The first "-s" provides only the grand total for all files. The second "-a" causes an entry to be generated for each file.

Example:

(1) Let's first try the command with no options.

```
user   ->   du /rlg/dick<r>
```

UNIX –>   24

```
24      /rlg/dick/.calendars
479     /rlg/dick/bin
12      /rlg/dick/.directories
532     /rlg/dick/awssim/onyx/interp
16      /rlg/dick/awssim/onyx/h
36      /rlg/dick/awssim/onyx/common
41      /rlg/dick/awssim/onyx/lib
643     /rlg/dick/awssim/onyx
1233    /rlg/dick/awssim
9       /rlg/dick/.ticklers
166     /rlg/dick/simdoc
43      /rlg/dick/working
392     /rlg/dick/onyx
274     /rlg/dick/reldata
30      /rlg/dick/source/new/yard/libr
89      /rlg/dick/source/new/yard/yard
123     /rlg/dick/source/new/yard
124     /rlg/dick/source/new
1       /rlg/dick/source/staging
90      /rlg/dick/source/stdio
224     /rlg/dick/source
25      /rlg/dick/library
333     /rlg/dick/book
136     /rlg/dick/atlas.tests
135     /rlg/dick/templet
2       /rlg/dick/play-work
89      /rlg/dick/newbook
302     /rlg/dick/emap.man
3932    /rlg/dick
```

–> $

In this example we were given the block count for each directory and the total for all the directories.

(2) Let's look at the command with the option "-a".

```
user   ->    du -a /rlg/dick/book<r>
UNIX  ->
```

```
13    /rlg/dick/book/appdx.a
27    /rlg/dick/book/chapt.1
23    /rlg/dick/book/chapt.2
19    /rlg/dick/book/chapt.3
17    /rlg/dick/book/chapt.4
21    /rlg/dick/book/chapt.5
16    /rlg/dick/book/chapt.6
16    /rlg/dick/book/chapt.7
29    /rlg/dick/book/chapt.8
14    /rlg/dick/book/chapt.9
2     /rlg/dick/book/doit
38    /rlg/dick/book/steve.mac
7     /rlg/dick/book/table.n
1     /rlg/dick/book/title.n
32    /rlg/dick/book/comm
37    /rlg/dick/book/comm.fmt
16    /rlg/dick/book/status
329   /rlg/dick/book
```

```
->    $
```

Each file in the directory book is listed and the number of blocks are given on the left-hand side. As we can see, we have 329 blocks used by all the files in directory "book".

(3)   Now let's try it with the option "-s".

```
user   ->    du -s /rlg/dick/book<r>
```

UNIX ->   329 /rlg/dick/book
      -> $

In this case only the total is provided.

Summary:

This command is useful when disk space is at a premium and you want to know which files and/or directories can have the most effect if deleted. Again this command is described in chapter 9.

7.4.8. Disk Free Space

Command:	df
Syntax:	df [file system]
Function:	This command provides a printout of the number of blocks available on the selected file system. It is generally used by the systems administrator; however, any time you think the system is getting low on storage you can check to see how many blocks are still free (see chapter 9 on the administration of a UNIX system).
Option:	No options exist for this command.

Example:

(1) On this particular system there exist two file systems. They are called rp1 and rp3. To find the number of available blocks of data on file system rp3 we simply say:

user   ->   df /dev/rp3<r>

```
UNIX  ->    /dev/rp3 6346
      ->    $
```

In this case the file system rp3 has 6346 blocks of free space still available for use.

Summary:

As we can see, we must know the file system's name before we can obtain information about its available space. In addition to this we must provide the information that it is a special file (information about it can be found in the directory "dev").

7.4.9. Determine File Type

Command:	file
Syntax:	file filename. . .
Function:	This command performs a series of tests on each filename provided and attempts to classify it. The file can be ascii, object, c programs, etc.
Option:	There are no options with this command.

Example:

(1) Let's try a few cases and see the results.

```
user  ->    file prog.c prog.o status doit<r>
UNIX  ->    prog.c: c program
      ->    prog.o: executable
      ->    status: roff, nroff, or eqn input
      ->    doit: commands
      ->    $
```

We have four (4) files here. The first is a c program, the second is an object module, the third is a nroff file, and the fourth is a set of UNIX commands. In this example the command was able to get all of them correctly. However there will be cases where it is not sure and will guess wrong.

Summary:

This command is useful when you are not sure of the contents of a file, although it is wise to look carefully because of the mistakes possible when using it.

7.4.10. Print Calendar

Command:	cal
Syntax:	cal [month] year
Function:	This command prints the calendar for a given month within a year or for a complete year. The year must be given and can be between 1 and 9999. This means that if you say 81, you will get the year 81 and not 1981.
Option:	There is one option and it specifies the month. It can be between 1 and 12.

Example:

(1) First let's ask for the calendar for 1981. We say:

```
user   ->   cal 1981<r>
UNIX  ->
```

1981

```
Jan                          Feb                          Mar
S  M Tu W Th  F  S           S  M Tu W Th  F  S           S  M Tu W Th  F  S
            1  2  3           1  2  3  4  5  6  7           1  2  3  4  5  6  7
 4  5  6  7  8  9 10          8  9 10 11 12 13 14           8  9 10 11 12 13 14
11 12 13 14 15 16 17         15 16 17 18 19 20 21          15 16 17 18 19 20 21
18 19 20 21 22 23 24         22 23 24 25 26 27 28          22 23 24 25 26 27 28
25 26 27 28 29 30 31                                      29 30 31

Apr                          May                          Jun
S  M Tu W Th  F  S           S  M Tu W Th  F  S           S  M Tu W Th  F  S
          1  2  3  4                        1  2           1  2  3  4  5  6
 5  6  7  8  9 10 11          3  4  5  6  7  8  9           7  8  9 10 11 12 13
12 13 14 15 16 17 18         10 11 12 13 14 15 16          14 15 16 17 18 19 20
19 20 21 22 23 24 25         17 18 19 20 21 22 23          21 22 23 24 25 26 27
26 27 28 29 30              24 25 26 27 28 29 30          28 29 30
                            31

Jul                          Aug                          Sep
S  M Tu W Th  F  S           S  M Tu W Th  F  S           S  M Tu W Th  F  S
          1  2  3  4                              1           1  2  3  4  5
 5  6  7  8  9 10 11          2  3  4  5  6  7  8           6  7  8  9 10 11 12
12 13 14 15 16 17 18          9 10 11 12 13 14 15          13 14 15 16 17 18 19
19 20 21 22 23 24 25         16 17 18 19 20 21 22          20 21 22 23 24 25 26
26 27 28 29 30 31           23 24 25 26 27 28 29          27 28 29 30
                            30 31

Oct                          Nov                          Dec
S  M Tu W Th  F  S           S  M Tu W Th  F  S           S  M Tu W Th  F  S
            1  2  3           1  2  3  4  5  6  7                 1  2  3  4  5
 4  5  6  7  8  9 10          8  9 10 11 12 13 14           6  7  8  9 10 11 12
11 12 13 14 15 16 17         15 16 17 18 19 20 21          13 14 15 16 17 18 19
18 19 20 21 22 23 24         22 23 24 25 26 27 28          20 21 22 23 24 25 26
25 26 27 28 29 30 31        29 30                         27 28 29 30 31
```

-> $

(2) Now let's see how to see the calendar for a given month.

```
user   ->   cal 1 1981<r>
UNIX  ->
```

```
      Jan 1981
      S  M Tu  W Th  F  S
                     1  2  3
       4  5  6  7  8  9 10
      11 12 13 14 15 16 17
      18 19 20 21 22 23 24
      25 26 27 28 29 30 31
```

```
UNIX  ->   $
```

Summary:

We can see that this command, as with the date command, provides an easy way in which to view any month or year. However, we must be exact with the year.

7.4.11. Questions

(1) How do you see where you are in the file system?

(2) How do you find out how many blocks are left in the file system "usr"?

(3) You don't have a watch available, and need to know the time. How do you find out by using the computer?

(4) How can you tell what name you are logged in as?

(5) Provide the active process ID numbers for all users.

(6) Provide the calendar for the year 1981?

7.5. Terminal Handling

The terminal handling commands allow you to view the current setting on your terminal and make changes as dictated by the terminal itself. There exist many different terminals and it would be impossible to use all of them without the capability to adjust as dictated by any given terminal.

7.5.1. Setting a Terminal

Command: stty

Syntax: stty [option. . .]

Function: This command allows you to view any terminal on the system and then set it up based on the options so that it will work on this system. It provides for such commands as input/output speed, parity, etc.

Option: The following options can be used with the stty command to set or unset the I/O options for a given terminal.

even	turn even parity to on
-even	turn even parity off
odd	turn odd parity to on
-odd	turn odd parity to off
raw	turn on raw mode input
-raw	turn off raw mode input
nl	Accept only new-line to end lines
-nl	allow return key for new line
echo	echo back each character typed
-echo	do not echo back each character typed
lcase	map upper case to lower case

-lcase	do not map to lower case
tabs	save tabs
-tabs	replace tabs by spaces when printing
ek	reset erase and kill characters back to normal # and @
erase	set erase character to next character typed after erase option.
kill	set kill character to next character after kill option
cr[0123]	select style of delay for carriage return
nl[0123]	select style of delay for linefeed
tab[0123]	select style of delay for tab
ff0 ff1	select style of delay for form feed
bs0 bs1	select style of delay for backspace
tty33	set all modes suitable for the Teletype Corporation Model 33 terminal
tty37	set all modes suitable for the Teletype Corporation Model 37 terminal
vt05	set all modes suitable for the Digital Equipment Corp. VT05 terminal
tn300	set all modes suitable for a General Electric TermiNet 300
ti700	set all modes suitable for a Texas Instruments 700 series terminal
tek	set all modes suitable for a Tektronix 4014 terminal
hup	hang up dataphone on last close
-hup	do not hang up dataphone on last close
0	hang up phone line immediately 50 75 110 134 150 200 300 600 1200 1800 2400 4800 9600 exta extb set terminal baud rate to the number given, if possible.

Example:

(1) Let's first view the setting on our terminal.

    user   −>   **stty\<r\>**

```
UNIX  ->    speed 1200 baud
      ->    erase = '#'; kill = '@'
      ->    even odd -nl echo -tabs tab2 ff1
      ->    $
```

We can see that the following options are set for this terminal.

1) baud rate is 1200

2) the erase character is "#"

3) the kill character is "@"

4) even parity is on

5) odd parity is on

6) return key is used for new-line

7) the characers are echoed back to the terminal

8) tabs are replaced by spaces when printing

9) the tab delay

10) the form feed delay

If need be we can change any of these options by simply including them after the stty command.

(2) Next let's look at the way in which we set another terminal.

```
user   ->    stty 9600 >/dev/tty2<r>
UNIX   ->    $
```

If you want to make sure that it has been set to 9600 baud, you can issue the "stty>/dev/tty2" command and it will show you what is set. This is an example of when you will need to know the terminal number before setting it. You will generally use this format when setting a printer terminal for printing.

(3) Another common change is for the erase character. The system always defaults to the erase character "#" when you login. However when you are using a crt you may want to use the backspace character instead of the "#". To set it we need only say:

```
user   ->   stty erase{bkspc}<r>
UNIX  ->   $
```

It appears as though we did not provide a character for the erase option. However the backspace on the key board when struck backs up one
space. And although you cannot see it it is there (one of the non printable
characters).

Summary:

This command is necessary whenever you have a new terminal and
have to set it up for use. There will also be times when you need to change
the baud rate for remote entry or for printing or whatever.

7.5.2. Setting The Terminal Tabs

Command: tabs

Syntax: tabs [option]

Function: This command allows us to set the tabs on
                   a variety of terminals as defined in "options".
                   However the default is suitable for most 300 baud
                   terminals.

Option: Two options exist for this command. They are:

-n   This is present when the left margin is not in-
                   dented as in normal.

terminal   The following terminals can be identified by the
                   system and the proper tab settings made.

Example:

(1) To set the tabs for a DIABLO 1620 we say:

```
user   ->    tabs 1620<r>
UNIX  ->    $
```

The system will get the proper settings for the DIABLO 1620 and make the settings.

Summary:

If the terminal you have is not one of the ones listed in the options under terminals, you will have to have your system administrator set up a new terminal description in the system.

7.5.3. Questions

(1) You have a printer connected to your computer and its current baud setting is 9600. How do you change it to 1200 baud (printer is tty3 and you are on tty1)?

(2) What is the advantage to using the option -tabs on the stty command?

(3) You have a diablo 1620 terminal. How can you set the tabs on it?

8. The UNIX Shell

To this point in our discussion we have talked about using one UNIX command at a time or tying them together with a pipe or temporary file. Now we will look at using a file which will contain several UNIX commands and perform a task the same as if we were entering them one at a time. There will be occasions when you will find yourself entering a series of commands to perform a particular task time after time. The advantage to entering it one time and placing it in a shell file will become very apparent. In addition to being able to place UNIX commands in a shell file, you will be able to control them to some extent with a simple set of constructs similar to those found in programming languages. The reason they are called shell files is that they are executed under control of the shell program which runs under UNIX. Other than that they look like any other file.

8.1. Simple Shell Files

There will be times when you find that you are entering the same set of commands over and over again to perform a task. If it's only a simple command there is no problem. However as the command gets more complex or involves more than one command it is time to start thinking about using shell files. Another reason is to provide a simple methodology for none UNIX users to perform complicated tasks without having to know

181

the details of all the commands.

A shell file consists of one or more UNIX commands that can perform a specific task. The file itself is created by using the editor and entering the commands just as you would directly on your terminal. The difference is that this file of commands can be executed any number of times by simply entering the name of the file.

Let's create a small shell file that will generate a list of the files in a selected directory and provide a count of the number of lines, words, and characters for each file. To execute this command directly on your terminal you would enter "cd work;wc *". To use it from a shell file we must first create a file "count" that will contain the commands "cd work;wc *". We use the editor "ed" to accomplish this first task.

Now that it is created, we can execute it in one of two ways. The first is to use the "sh" command followed by the file name. This will cause the commands in the file to be executed as though they were coming directly from the terminal. The second is to change the mode of the file to execute by use of the chmod command.

Example:

```
user    ->    ed count<r>
ED      ->    ?count
user    ->    a<r>
        ->    cd work; wc *<r>
        ->    .<r>
        ->    w<r>
ED      ->    7
user    ->    q<r>
UNIX    ->    $
```

We have now created the shell file "count" which when executed will produce a count of the lines, words, and characters for all files in your directory "work".

Now let's execute it using the "sh" command.

```
user    ->    sh count<r>
```

```
UNIX  ->    7 21 83 file1
      ->    7 21 83 file2
      ->    7 21 83 file3
      ->    1 5 11 table1
      ->    1 5 11 table2
      ->    6 6 34 x
      ->    29 79 305 total
      ->    $
```

Now, if we change the mode to execute by use of the command "chmod 0777 count", we can execute it without having to use the shell command.

```
user  ->    count<r>
UNIX  ->    7 21 83 file1
      ->    7 21 83 file2
      ->    7 21 83 file3
      ->    1 5 11 table1
      ->    1 5 11 table2
      ->    6 34 x
      ->    29 79 305 total
      ->    $
```

This is useful if the results are always coming from the directory "work"; however, it is not very flexible. The next section covers how we can make these shell commands a little more powerful by use of arguments.

8.1.1. Shell Files and Arguments

Using the same example from the previous section we can extend its capability to handle selected directories by use of an argument in the calling sequence. This is somewhat like the use of options in a single command.

An argument in a shell file is represented by the use of the symbol "$n", where n can have the value 1 to 9. Thus you can use up to nine(9) arguments in a shell file.

In the previous section we could only obtain the counts for files in directory "work". Let's now use our knowledge of arguments to allow the user to select the directory that is to be used.

All we need do is replace the directory name "work" with the argument symbol "$1". This tells us that we must supply the name of the directory at the time we invoke the shell file. Thus our new shell file will contain "cd $1; wc *". We can then execute it as follows:

```
user   ->    count work<r>
UNIX   ->     7 21 83 file1
       ->     7 21 83 file2
       ->     7 21 83 file3
       ->     1  5 11 table1
       ->     1  5 11 table2
       ->     6  6 34 x
       ->    29 79 305 total
       ->    $
```

As we can see, the results are the same, but we were able to select the directory at the time we invoked the shell file. Next let's expand our shell file to allow us to also produce the count for only those files we select at the time we execute it. Thus our new shell file will contain "cd $1; wc $2". Now we have to supply two arguments, with the first one always being the directory and the second being the file or pattern that we want. To execute it we say:

```
user   ->    count work file?<r>
UNIX   ->     7 21 83 file1
       ->     7 21 83 file2
       ->     7 21 83 file3
       ->    21 63 249 total
       ->    $
```

We have asked only for those files that start with "file" and have only one additional character which can be any legal character.

8.1.2. Nesting Shell Files

The ability to nest shell files exists in UNIX. Arguments are handled the same way as with a single shell file. There exist many uses for this capability, with one common usage being:

Example:

(1) Create a master shell file that controls the function of several local shell files. In this case we have four shell files, each controlling the functions of a local directory. The master shell file is used to invoke all of the others. You could invoke each of the local shell files independently, but it is much easier to invoke them all at the same time.

In this example the local shell files will provide us with a list of the files in a specific directory and then the line count for each file in that directory.

shell1 contains:	shell2 contains:	shell3 contains:
file1	filea	filex
file2	fileb	filey
file3	filec	filez
in dir dick/A	in dir dick/B	in dir dick/C

Then the master shell file will be:

```
master contains:
cd dick/A
echo shell1
shell1
cd ../B
echo shell2
shell2
cd ../C
echo shell3
shell3
echo done
```

To execute this master shell procedure, you will have to change the mode to execute on each of the shell files and make sure that you have permission to execute them (i.e., they belong to you). If not you can call each of them by use of the command "sh". We could make this more flexible by passing arguments indicating what directories should be used.

8.2. Use of Variables

Another useful capability in the use of shell procedures is the use of variables. They provide you with the ability to assign string-valued variables. These variable names must begin with a letter and consist only of letters, digits and underscores. The string cannot contain blanks.

Example:

Let's first try a simple shell procedure that echo's some messages to the terminal after some event.

The procedure (print) will look as follows:

```
A=first_time
B=second_time
C=third_time

echo $A
echo $B
echo $C

echo that's it folks
```

```
user   ->    sh print<r>
UNIX   ->    first_time
UNIX   ->    second_time
UNIX   ->    third_time
UNIX   ->    that's all folks
```

We can also assign pathnames to a variable.

In this case we will change directories to another one, execute the shell file "print" in that directory and then change back to the current directory.

The shell file "print" is in the previous directory (one level back) and we will execute the following shell file called "xx".

```
Path1=../
Path2=current

cd $Path1
sh print
cd $Path2
echo finished
```

To execute this procedure and see the results we say:

```
user   ->   sh print<r>
UNIX  ->   first_time
UNIX  ->   second_time
UNIX  ->   third_time
UNIX  ->   that's all folks
UNIX  ->   finished
```

This example is very useful for a number of reasons, one being that you can execute shell files in other directories, but the most important one is that you set up pathname that have special meaning to you. Let's show an example of what we mean.

The following variables have a special meaning to the shell and should be avoided for general use.

$MAIL — When the shell is used interactively, it will look at the file specified by this variable before it issues a prompt. If the specified file has been modified since it was last looked at the shell prints the message "you have mail" before prompting for the next command.

Chapter 8

$HOME   This is the default argument for the cd command. The current directory is used to resolve file name references that do not begin with a "/". The HOME directory is the directory specified by the login reference found in the password file.

$PATH   A list of directories that contain commands (the search path). This provides you with the capability to search selected directories for information which are different than the standard directories which are "/bin and /usr/bin".

These special variables are generally set in a ".profile" file located in your home directory. This file is executed automatically each time you login. This can allow you to setup any conditions you may desire each time you enter the system. By doing it this way instead of invoking it directly, you eliminate the chance that you might forget.

Example:

Let's set up a shell procedure that will be executed automatically each time you login. It will perform the following functions:

1) Search my bin file as well as /bin and /usr/bin.

2) Change the backspace character from # to backspace key.

The shell file must be named ".profile" or the system will not automatically invoke it.

```
stty erase
echo backspace is backspace key
PATH=:/usr/dick/bin:/bin:/usr/bin
```

The path also defines the order in which the system will search the designated directories. In this case, /usr/dick/bin will be searched first.

The stty command doesn't display the backspace key because it is an invisible character, but it is there.

8.3. Summary

We have only lightly touched on the capabilities of the shell. However this will provide you with enough information to perform many of the simpler (and more common) tasks. Once you have confidence in this then you can move on to the more complicated procedures.

8.4. Questions

(1)   What is a shell file and what is its value?

(2)   How many arguments are allowed in a shell file?

(3)   Show an example of nested shell files.

(4)   What variables are restricted from general use?

9. SYSTEM ADMINISTRATOR

9.1. Introduction to System Administration

The system administrator is the person at a computer installation who is responsible for day-to-day operation of the machine. This includes bringing the system up and down when necessary; adding new users to the system and removing obsolete users; taking tape dumps of the file system so that files will be recoverable in case of a disaster; running accounting programs that tell you who is using how much computer time and disk space; and generally making sure that the system operates as smoothly as possible. Other responsibilities include keeping the system log book. This book should reflect anything that is done to the system along the lines of bringing it up or down; any hardware changes – permanent or temporary; and device or file system errors that are discovered.

9.1.1. Privileged Users

There are at least two privileged users on the system who have special powers and abilities beyond those of ordinary users. One of these is called the "superuser" – the actual login name is "root", but the term

190

superuser is common usage in UNIX terminology. The superuser can do almost anything conceivable to the system or the file structure. The other, less privileged special user is called "bin", and does not have any special privileges directly. However, "bin" owns many important system files, and as a result of this can do things to those files that nobody else except the superuser can do.

The superuser is a truly formidable user. No file protections affect him/her (with a couple of trivial and accidental exceptions); the superuser can read and write anybody's files or directories. However, as a wise man once said: "With great power, there must also come great responsibility." The superuser can, by making a tiny mistake, destroy the entire file system, cripple it so that the operating system will not run, and make a general mess of the system. For instance, the superuser could effectively bring down the system by doing this:

```
user   ->    chdir /bin
       ->    rm *
UNIX   ->    #
```

If you do this, no ordinary system programs will run. This includes the programs that the superuser uses to fix the system. If you were foolish enough to make this mistake, you would have to bring down the system, restore your root file system from a backup (a complicated undertaking), and explain to your superior that you had messed up. You probably want to avoid this. On the other hand, even the most expert and high-minded superuser eventually makes a mistake, so don't become despondent if (when) you do mess up. If you follow the other procedures in this chapter – particularly those relating to backup of file systems for use in case of disaster – you can recover from the most moronic of errors with not too much work lost.

Note, by the way, the prompt "#" – as opposed to the normal UNIX prompt "$".

This is the superuser prompt, and it reminds you that you are indeed the superuser and have awesome power. Because of the power of the superuser, you are advised to keep the number of people who know the password down to two – yourself and somebody who is to use it only in case of emergency – that is, if you yourself are unavailable.

There are two ways to become the superuser. One is to login as user named "root" and give the right password. The other is to run the program "su" from the shell. You must give the password in this case as well. When you are done as superuser, type a control-D and you will be either logged out (if you logged in as "root") or returned to your normal privileges (if you ran "su"). Also, when the system is first "booted up" and is still running in single-user mode, you have superuser powers (this is explained further under "Booting The System" below).

Coming up superuser using root or su.

```
UNIX  ->   login:
user  ->   root<r>
UNIX  ->   password:
user  ->   <r>              enter password, no echo
UNIX  ->   #                This is superuser prompt
```

To use su, you must already be logged in.

```
UNIX  ->   $                normal user prompt
user  ->   su<r>
UNIX  ->   password:
user  ->   <r>              enter password, no echo
UNIX  ->   #                This is superuser prompt
```

The other privileged user is called "bin". It has no special privileges in the sense that the superuser does; however, "bin" owns all of the programs in /bin and /usr/bin, and usually the devices (special files) such as the terminals, and the printer. In general any "system-owned" file will be owned either by "root" (the superuser) or by "bin". As system administrator you will be able to be logged in as both "root" and "bin". If you can do what you have to do by logging in only as "bin" rather than as "root", you should do so; the less time you spend as superuser, the less accidental damage you can do. To log in as bin, you do the same as shown above with root.

A word of philosophy: in this section it may seem to you that we are being pessimistic about your abilities, inasmuch as we have repeatedly assumed that you at some point will make some horrible mistake. This is no reflection on the individual administrator; computer programmers are simply aware from unpleasant personal experience of the well-known Murphy's Law: "Anything that can go wrong, will." The most brilliant programmers have done the stupidest things in the past, often from overconfidence in their ability to operate the system. It just seems to be a fact of life: at some point something bad will happen, in spite of the expertise of the people involved, and sometimes because of their expertise. This is why all of the warnings in this guide are here; it is also why we strongly advise a policy of being prepared for disaster.

9.1.2. Adding New Users

Let us turn our attention to some simple tasks that you will have to perform and that do not require too much specialized knowledge to perform. For a start, let us see how to add a new user to the system.

The complete system list of users is the file /etc/passwd, known as the "password file". Each line in this file contains an entry for one user. For instance, the first few lines of a typical /etc/passwd might be:

root:ty2IuAdu:0:1:Super-User:/:

su::0:1:Super-User:/:

daemon::1:1:System:/usr/1115:

bin::3:1:System:/bin:

opr::3:1:Operator:/usr/adm:

dump::3:1:System:/usr/adm:/usr/adm/dumper

games::26:1:Games:/usr/games:

dick:nnAnXu4n:92:2:Dick Gauthier:/rlg/dick:

roy:jjtx62bk:68:2:Roy Oishi:/rlg/roy:

lea:NYr2Njzk:11:5:Lea Gallardo:rlg/lea:

The fields in each line – separated by colons – are as follows: the login name; the encrypted form of the user's password (not the password itself); the user id; the group id; the user's full name, (or other comment), the login directory – that is, the directory in which the user finds him/herself immediately upon logging in; and the user's shell (command interpreter). If this last field is left out, the ordinary UNIX shell is used. The user "dump" in the above example is a pseudo-user who runs only the program /usr/adm/dumper when s/he logs in; when this program finishes "dump" is logged out. The user id and the group id are numbers between 0 and 255. Each user should have a distinct user id number; related users (those working on the same project) should have the same group id. The group-id file, analogous to /etc/passwd, is /etc/group.

To add a new user, you simply add a new line to /etc/passwd. The new line will look like the above lines, with one important note: the password field must be left empty. This indicates to UNIX that the user has no password. When the user logs in for the first time, s/he should use the "passwd" (See chapter 2) to give him/herself a password; this program will take care of changing /etc/passwd to reflect the change.

user	->	ed /etc/passwd\<r>	You must have write permission
ED	->	1234	
user	->	$ \<r>	go to end of file
user	->	a \<r>	enter add mode
user	->	sam::12:1:Sam Jones:/usr/sam:\<r>	
user	->	. \<r>	exit add mode
user	->	w\<r>	write changes out to file
ED	->	1264	
user	->	q \<r>	
UNIX	->	#	

If, as is generally done, you have named a directory that does not yet exist as the new user's login directory, you must create this directory before the user can log in. Use mkdir as described in chapter 7, then change the ownership of the directory from "root" to the new user's, as described in the following section.

user	->	cd /usr\<r>	position at root directory
UNIX	->	#	
user	->	mkdir sam \<r>	must match dir name in passwd file

```
UNIX  ->   #                          you must have write permis-
                                      sion
```

9.1.3. Changing File Ownership and Protection

Other easy functions that you will have to perform include changing ownership and protection information. To change the ownership of a file, you must be the superuser. The command for changing ownership is simply:

#chown USERNAME FILENAME

– where USERNAME is the login name of the user, the file is to be owned by, and FILENAME is of course the name of the file.

Similarly, you can change any file's group-association with

#chgrp GROUPNAME FILENAME

– where GROUPNAME is a group name listed in /etc/group.

```
user   ->   chgrp 1 sam<r>
UNIX  ->   #
```

Let us review at this point the meaning of the protections on a file. There are nine bits of protection information; they represent the ability to read, write, and execute a file; such abilities being for the user her/himself, those in the group associated with the file, and all others – thus, nine combinations. If you type "ls -l" you can see this on the left-hand side:

```
user   ->   ls -l<r>
UNIX  ->
```

```
-rwxr-xr-x   1 dick    25102   Apr 6 15:11    3dcomp
-rw-rw-rw-   1 dick     7548   Sep 16 15:37   iii
-rwsr-sr-x   1 root     3322   Apr 8 1976     passwd
```

drwxr-xr-x	2 dick	256	Sep 21 15:55	sacourse
drwxrwxr-x	2 root	512	Dec 18 09:24	book
-rw-r-r-	1 dick	83	Oct 15 17:03	file1
-rw-r-r-	1 dick	83	Oct 19 13:31	file2
-rw-r-r-	1 dick	83	Oct 19 13:44	file3
-rw-r-r-	1 dick	83	Oct 22 18:43	filen
-rw-r-r-	1 dick	82	Oct 19 12:18	sfile1
-rw-r-r-	1 dick	83	Oct 15 17:05	sfile2
-rw-r-r-	1 dick	82	Oct 19 13:47	sfile3
-rw-r-r-	1 dick	11	Oct 15 15:45	table1
-rw-r-r-	1 dick	11	Oct 15 15:45	table2
-rw-rw-r-	1 dick	11	Oct 15 15:45	table3
-rw-rw-r-	1 dick	11	Oct 15 15:45	table4

For most files here, the owner (dick) can read and write them, but those in his group and all others can only read them; for the file "iii", everybody – user, group members, and others – can both read and write. The file "3dcomp" is a program and is marked executable by anyone. The file "sacourse" is a directory. The fact that it is a directory is shown by "ls" as a 'd' at the left of the protection bits. Don't misinterpret this – there is no 'd' bit, and you can't make a file a directory by changing its protection; "ls" just chooses to display the information in this way.

There is one final protection possibility; programs with the "set-uid" bit on will execute with their "effective user id" the same as the owner's. Thus, if the superuser owns a program that requires his powers to run, but he wants to let everybody use it, he can set the set-uid bit of the program; then whoever runs it can do what the superuser could do until the program ends. For example, look at the program "passwd", in the above list, which is used to change a user's password. The passwd program requires the set-uid feature because in order to change the /etc/passwd file, the effective user-id must be that of "root"; when an ordinary user runs this program it is as if (s)he temporarily becomes "root". When the program is done, all is set back to normal. Note, by the way, that the set-uid bit displays on the "ls -l" listing as an 's' in the 'x'-bit position. Don't be misled by this; the set-uid bit is separate from the execute bit. The "ls" program just chooses to put the 's' there (perhaps the author of "ls" thought it would only make sense with the 'x' bit on; we should know better).

Some of the permission bits have slightly different meanings for directories than for plain files (in some senses, a directory is a file). For directories, the 'x' bit means "search permission"; if a user cannot search a directory (s)he cannot "chdir" to it or access any file under it in any way. Write permission for a directory means the ability to add, remove, or rename files in the directory. Thus, permission to remove a file is independent of permission to write it or make it empty. User programs (even for the super-user) cannot write to a directory as though it were an ordinary file. Read permission for the directory works as with plain files; it allows the directory to be read. The "ls" program reads directories to obtain filenames. Note that the ability to read a file is independent of the ability to read its name.

To change a file's protections, use the "chmod" command:

$ chmod OCTAL-# FILENAME

The octal number is formed as follows: the digits from left to right are the "user", "group", and "everybody" protections. Each digit is the sum of 1 for execute/search permission, 2 for write permission, and 4 for read permission. Thus to let a file be readable by all and writable by you alone, issue:

```
user   ->    chmod 644 FILENAME<r>
UNIX  ->    $
```

This will result in a uid setting of '-rw-r--r-'.

To set the set-uid bit, prefix the protection number with '4'; prefixing by '2' instead will turn on the "set-gid" bit, which is like the set-uid bit but works by groups. (Prefixing by '6' will set both of these bits.) In order to change a file's protections you must either own it or be the superuser.

9.2. Introduction to System Components

This section tells about the basic components of your system – the hardware, a brief idea of the different categories of software, and a brief introduction to "file systems".

9.2.1. Hardware

The basic hardware of your system includes a mainframe, otherwise known as "the computer"; one or more disk drives, which hold all of your system's data; several terminals of one sort or another, either typewriter-like or video-display; a line printer, which is an output-only device; and a tape drive, which reads and writes tapes.

9.2.1.1. The Mainframe

The mainframe is the central unit of your system. It contains a Central Processing Unit (CPU) and the computer's primary memory. The processor is the active component that executes programs by copying the program into its memory and then performing the machine instructions that make up the program. In addition, the CPU's operator console – the front panel and its switches – is the means by which the machine is started and stopped. The operator's console is different for each Computer and requires reading the instructions provided with it.

9.2.1.2. The Disk Drive(s)

Every UNIX system has at least one disk drive, each of which in turn contains one or more disks inside the drive. There are various sorts of drives: they can have non-removable disks, or they can have removable disks and be front-loading drives, or they can have removable disks and be top-loading drives. A disk can contain between 2.5 and over 100 megabytes, depending on the kind of drive. (A megabyte is one million bytes or characters.) The "transfer rate" – the speed with which data can be read or written – also varies with the disk model. Every model of disk drive has its own set of lights and buttons, but most have some combination of the following:

READY	This light should be on for system operation.
FAULT	This means a serious hardware error: you may need hardware repairs.

LOAD   This light means that you may remove a disk.

PROT   This means that the disk cannot be written on; to clear it push the button containing or corresponding to the light.

The disk is used to contain all data in the system when that data is not being actively processed. This includes not only data that programs operate on but the programs themselves – when you ask for a program to be run UNIX arranges for a file with that name to be read from the disk into the main memory and be executed.

A word here on the care of your drives and disks: a single particle of dust that gets into the drive can ruin the disk. The drive is amazingly sensitive to such things. Care should be taken that no dust or other particles get in by any means; you are advised not to smoke or eat in the machine room.

Disk drives are generally numbered 0,1,. . . so that the processor can tell them apart. If you have more than one drive, it is useful to be able to change the association of numbers to drives during emergencies (see the section on Using a Backup Copy of UNIX). On some types of disk drives, this may be accomplished by simply exchanging the unit number plugs – the plastic covers for the "ready" lights. On other types of drives, cables must be changed around.

9.2.1.3. Terminals

You will have one or more types of terminals, which are the major point of contact between users and the computer. The terminals come in a variety of flavors; you may have a CRT (tv-screen) terminal; you may have a hard-copy terminal, which prints its output onto paper directly; and/or you may have a Diablo-like terminal which produces high-quality output that "doesn't look like a computer did it" and is suitable for business correspondence. Your terminals probably have an "online/ofline" or "online/local" switch, which must be in the "online" position in order to communicate with the machine. In addition, different terminals run at different speeds, possibly controlled by a switch on the terminal. In order for UNIX to know the type and speed of the terminal on each line, there is a file that contains that information; the updating of this file is the system administrator's responsibility and will be explained in a later section.

9.2.1.4. The Line Printer

The line printer is usually your major hard-copy device. The most important things to note about it are the lights and buttons. There is an online/offline button and a corresponding indicator light that tells whether or not the printer is listening to the computer. If this light is off, the printer is not going to print anything – on the other hand, the computer knows when the printer isn't listening, so it waits until the printer is on line again. When the printer is off-line, you can hit the "top-of-form" button and the printer will eject a page. There are several error indicators, such as "paper", "gate", and "ribbon", that go on when something goes physically wrong with printer operation. (You may have to lift up the printer cover to see these.) When the "alarm" light on the printer panel goes on, one or more of these error lights will also be on. Fix the problem indicated, and push the "alarm" button – this clears the error state. Now push the "online" button to bring the printer back on line; the printer should start up with as little loss of output as possible. There is another problem that sometimes happens with the printer on some systems – the printer just sits for a while without printing, for no apparent reason. This is described as "the printer is stuck", and it is a software problem, not a hardware problem. You can unstick the printer in 30 seconds from any UNIX terminal, but that will be described later on (see "unsticking the line printer" in a later section).

9.2.1.5. The Tape Drive

Tapes are the best way to store large amounts of data if the data is not in constant use. For example, tapes are used to save large portions of your disk file system on tape as insurance against disk disaster. Tapes are also the best facility for getting data or programs from one computer system to another.

Tape drives may have a data density of 800 bytes/inch (that is, characters/inch) or of 1600 bytes/inch. Some drives have a switch that selects which density is to be used, and a tape written with a given density must be read with that density. Another source of incompatibility is the number of tracks; there are 7-track and 9-track tape drives. Neither of these types of drive can read tapes written by the other. Many UNIX installations are capable of reading and writing only 9-track tapes.

Drives also vary in speed, but this only affects how fast things are read and written, and does not really affect operation in any other way – speed of writing and speed of reading need not be the same.

Again, there are several kinds of tape drive you may have; all of them work in almost the same way. To put a tape on the drive, you must take a tape and, if you are writing on it, there must be a plastic ring (called not unreasonably the "write ring") in the back of the tape reel. If on the other hand it's an important tape that you want to make sure you don't accidentally write over, there should be no write ring in the tape. The tape drive is incapable of writing on a tape which has no write ring.

Once you have a tape with the ring in or out as desired, put it on the empty hub. Thread it through to the take-up reel (follow the diagram on the drive) and see that it is firmly attached to the take-up reel. Now push "load". The tape will wander about looking for its "load point", which is just a bit of foil towards the start of the tape. The tape always starts here; in this way the beginning of the tape is found. Depending on your drive model, you may now have to push the "on line" button – do whatever you have to do to make the "on-line" light go on. The tape is now ready for use by a program. After you are done with the tape, push the "rewind" button. Depending on what has been done with the tape, the rewind will either go back to the load point, or, if it is already there, it will rewind the tape totally off the take-up reel; thus you may have to push the button twice to take the tape off.

9.2.2. Software

The software of a computer system is the collection of programs that run on it. The UNIX operating system has two general parts to its software. The first and most essential piece is called variously the "kernel" or "nucleus". The nucleus performs only the most basic functions of an operating system: it arranges for all of the input/output operations and it gives everybody their little pieces of computer time (this is called "scheduling" in the trade).

The rest of the software includes the Shell (the command interpreter) and the user commands. When you "boot" the system (described later), the boot mechanism takes the kernel off the disk (where it is stored) and reads it into memory. The machine can then start going. The kernel knows where the other software is and arranges for it to be invoked when users request it, but these other programs are not actually part of the kernel.

The commands and programs available to system users are simply files stored in the file system, mostly in the directories called "/bin" and "/usr/bin". (More on these directories and their significance later.) The system administrator can add programs to these directories, thus making them available for general use. By way of contrast, the kernel can only be changed by a UNIX specialist, and will only need to be changed if your installation gets new hardware of some sort, or if your pattern of system use changes and you find that you need new system resources.

Some important parameters in the UNIX kernel are:

- which disk (or part thereof) is to hold the root file system

- what part of which disk is to serve as swap space

9.2.3. File Systems – A Brief Look

A file system is a UNIX concept that you as system administrator will become quite familiar with. A file system is an organized group of files that fit either on all of one disk or, if you have larger disks than the maximum size of a UNIX file system, on part of a disk. (File systems never start on one disk and end on another.) You have one essential file system called the "root" file system; it contains the minimum needed to run UNIX. Other file systems are made accessible by "mounting" them onto the root directory structure, with the effect that what appears to the user to be an ordinary (though rather large) directory is in fact stored on a separate file system – though the ordinary user need not normally concern himself with this fact. For example, the entire directory "/usr" and all of its subdirectories may be a mounted file system on your computer.

This facility allows for some flexibility in using your system. You may want to have different file systems mounted at different times, for instance. Many system administration tasks are done in terms of whole file systems: taking tape dumps and checking disk integrity are the most important of these.

9.3. Starting and Stopping the System

This section explains how to start and stop UNIX. Whenever you do something like this it is your responsibility to enter everything that you do in the system log book.

9.3.1. Shutting Down the System

There are a number of times you might want to stop the machine. Your daily routine may provide for stopping the system at the end of the working day and starting it up again in the morning. If hardware maintenance to the mainframe or the disks is needed you will probably need to stop the system. If, at all possibl,e you should follow the procedure explained here to make sure that the file systems are not damaged during the shutdown process, and make the whole thing as painless as possible for your users.

The first thing to do is to become the superuser (see section 9.1 of this document). After this, you should alert all users to the impending shutdown by running

```
user    ->    enters      /etc/wall
        ->                (message here
        ->                any number of lines)
user    ->                <cntrl>d
UNIX    ->    #
```

– which will send the message you type to all logged-in terminals. If you have enough advance knowledge of the shutdown you ought to put a note to that effect in /etc/motd, the message-of-the-day file that is listed on the the terminal whenever a user logs in.

Having alerted users to the shutdown, you should keep running "who" (which lists all logged-in users) until all users except yourself have logged off. At this point run

```
user    ->    ps alx <r>
UNIX    ->
```

F	S	UID	PID	PPID	CPU	PRI	NICE	ADDR	SZ	WCHAN	TTY	TIME	CMD
1	S	0	1	0	0	30	20	74	12	11556	?	0:22	/etc/init
1	S	13	6908	1	0	28	20	135	16	107466	co	0:03	-sh
0	S	0	21	1	0	28	20	147	12	107632	1	0:00	- x
1	S	0	8	1	0	40	20	65	12	164000	?	7:05	/etc/update
1	S	1	10	1	0	40	20	155	28	164000	?	5:49	/etc/cron
1	S	0	19	1	0	40	20	71	12	164000	1p	0:01	/etc/openup
1	S	13	6675	1	0	28	20	61	16	107714	4	0:10	-sh
1	S	4	9214	1	0	30	20	141	16	12062	2	0:02	-sh
0	S	0	24	1	0	28	20	253	12	110060	5	0:00	-x
0	S	0	25	1	0	28	20	267	12	110224	6	0:00	-x
1	S	0	26	1	0	28	20	117	12	110370	co	0:00	-ps axl

– there should be no user processes running.

This means that there should be no named commands running except for the "update" process and whatever "daemons" have been started up by /etc/rc (which will be explained in a later section). If there are still some user processes around, either make sure that they end soon or kill them outright using the kill command described below.

Now perform the following three functions:

user   –>   kill -1 1<r>   (you can kill all processes ex-
                                       cept "init" (process 1) and
                                       bring the system back to
                                       single user mode)

user   –>   sync<r>

– and HALT the CPU –

At this point (after you have halted the CPU) the system has been gracefully halted. If at this point you are turning your system over to a hardware repairer, you should take steps to protect the contents of your disks against the repairer's mistakenly overwriting them. If you have removable disks, remove them. Otherwise have the data backed up to tape. Computer fixers have an amazing talent for stomping good data on disks.

9.3.2. Booting the System

"Booting" the system is a process that enables the computer to start operation. The reason for a "boot" procedure is as follows: when the machine is first started, there is no program running, nor is there one in memory. Thus the first thing to do is get a program into memory. Unfortunately, the program – the operating system kernel – is out there on the disk, and the processor doesn't know where it is; thus a program has to be put in the processor telling it how to get the operating system into memory. Now, there is no way to get this program off the disk because the processor doesn't know where it is or how to read it in because there is no program in memory ... you see the problem. Well, then, how does the system get started? The answer is that you must load in one tiny program that knows how to read in another program (a larger one) which in turn knows how to read in the operating system itself. This is called bootstrapping because it's like lifting yourself by your bootstraps.

If you have halted the machine as in the last section, you are in fact ready to boot. If the system "crashed" – meaning that something went wrong and the system has stopped while doing something useful – you must HALT the machine before booting (see the hardware description section of the manual for the computer you are using).

9.3.3. Booting Procedure

After going through the steps described in the "Booting the System" section above, type "boot" (and a line feed or carriage return; this is implied from here on). You should see a ":" prompt. The exact boot start procedure depends on the computer type. It could be as defined above or simply a button on the computer.

Then type a command of the form

xx(0,0)unix

where xx is the UNIX two-letter code for the type of disk you are booting from (this is not the same as the DEC two-letter codes described above for some processor models). Some of the codes are:

rp........RP03

hp........RP04/5/6
rk........RK05

When you get the "#" prompt, UNIX is up in single user mode.
Procede with the file system integrity check described below.

9.3.4. File Integrity Check – Simple Case

When the system is brought up single-user you should run file system integrity checking procedure (generally called "chk") which runs the
checking programs on each file system. These programs can detect inconsistencies in the file system and report what is wrong. Here is a typical
"chk":

dcheck /dev/rrp1

icheck /dev/rrp1

dcheck /dev/rrk3

icheck /dev/rrk3

This procedure should be run daily even if the system does not go
down, so that you are alerted to any problems before they get worse. Fixing
file systems can become complicated in dificult cases, but as long as your
hardware is in good shape the dificult cases should be rather rare. The
dificult cases will be dealt with in a later section; for the moment you should
just learn to recognize when the file system is healthy, as it usually is –
especially if you followed the recommended graceful shut-down procedure.

The output from the above "chk" procedure might look like this when
nothing is wrong:

/dev/rrp1:

/dev/rrp1:

files 542 (r=448,d=47,b=13,c=34)

used 8779 (i=212,ii=7,iii=0,d=8553)

free 6586

missing 0

/dev/rrp1:

/dev/rrp1:

/dev/rrp3:

/dev/rrp3:

files 1003 (r=934,d=69,b=0,c=0)

used 7564 (i=206,ii=0,iii=0,d=7358)

free 6834

missing 0

/dev/rrp3:

/dev/rrp3:

The general format of a normal output from "chk" is, for each file system, the device name of that system twice, followed by some of these entries: spcl, files, large, huge, direc, indir, used, and free (the "huge" entry can be missing). The following indicate ERROR output and some sort of file system problem: "missing", "dup", "dups in free", "bad freeblock", or anything at all between the two "/dev/whatever:" lines. Any discrepancies in the output should be fixed in acccordance with section 8 of this document.

Some UNIX systems have a check command. When this is available, it can handily take the place of the icheck and check commands invoked by the chk procedure mentioned above. If fcheck does not ask you any questions, everything is OK. Typical fcheck output for a healthy file system looks like this:

/fdev/root:

Phase 1 - Check Blocks

Phase 3 - Check Pathnames

Phase 4 - Check Reference Counts

Phase 5 - Check Free List

235 files   1713 blocks   2200 free

When all file system problems have been fixed, you are ready to bring UNIX up multi-user.

Coming up Multi-User

There are only a few things to do in order to bring up the system multi-user. First, set the system date.

You set the date on a UNIX system with a command of the form

#date yyMMddhhmm.ss

Where the two-digit fields are the year, month, day-of-month, hour, minute, and second. ".ss" can be omitted to specify zero seconds. The year, or the year and month can be omitted if these have not changed since the system was brought down. Hence, usually only the hours and minutes need be entered, for example:

user   ->   date 1321
UNIX ->   Mon Feb 16 13:21:58 PST 1981

for 21 minutes after 1 in the afternoon.

The system will then print out the date in a human-readable form to make sure that you entered it right – if it's wrong, fix it.

Next you might want to change /etc/motd to mention if there is anything the users ought to know – if files were lost, for example.

To do this simply enter the message in the file motd just as you would do with any other file. It is always located in the directory /etc.

Finally, type <cntrl>d. Within a few seconds, the shell file /etc/rc will be executed – this mounts the standard file systems and will be covered in more detail later –, all terminals will be enabled, and the system will be up multi-user. Again, don't forget to enter everything you did in the system log book.

9.4. System Resources and the Administrator

As system administrator you have the job of making sure that all users have a fair share of system resources. The principal resources that you need to worry about are disk space and processes.

9.4.1. Disk Space

Disk space is a resource that users don't worry about until they run out of it. The system administrator, on the other hand, has to worry about it before it runs out. If you do this properly, you should be able to avoid running out of disk space.

First you should know how much free space you need on your file systems. When your computer system is installed, you should be aware of about how much free storage is normal on your user file systems, and notice when the free space shrinks dramatically. You will probably want to keep about 15% of each file system free — less if a given file system doesn't change much, more if it does. The most unusual file system in this respect is the one containing the directory /tmp; this directory will start out the day empty and will fluctuate wildly during the day. It is recommended that you have at least 100 blocks of free storage per simultaneous user on /tmp.

Now you need to know the programs that detect a shortage of space. When you bring up the system and run the "chk" procedure (or fcheck, as applicable), you will find that under each file system there is a count of the free blocks. Running out of blocks will prevent any existing files from growing and new files from being created. You can determine how much free space there is by issuing the "df" command. This will tell you how many free blocks there are on any given file system. Between these two programs you can be warned when storage gets tight. If the console terminal ever starts typing:

No space on dev M/m

(with numbers in place of the M and m)

A file system has completely run out of space. It is best to avoid this if possible, for among the possible unpleasant consequences are damage to file system integrity, and users being unable to save their editing work.

Now: suppose you are running out of storage. What should you do? First of all, if you have a momentary shortage on /tmp, you can wait a minute and see if whoever is gobbling up the space stops whatever it is (s)he is doing. Some things that use /tmp space are: large sorting jobs, compiling programs, editing, and text processing; you may run into others. If the situation persists, you will have to delete some /tmp files – you may want to run "ls -lut /tmp", which lists all files on /tmp sorted in order of last access. This will show you which files have not been accessed for a while and could perhaps be deleted. If all else fails, you could bring down the system and start it again, which would clear the /tmp directory; but you shouldn't have to do this unless everything has ground to a halt as a result of a /tmp space shortage.

When you are running out of space on an ordinary user file system, first ask around to see if anybody admits to having generated thousands of blocks (possibly by accident) – /etc/wall is good for this. In conjunction with this you could alert people that space is tight and they should remove what files they can. If this fails, you will have to do some detective work. The programs "du" and "find" are both useful here. The program "du" simply tells you how many blocks are used by a given directory and all files and subdirectories in it. This can be used if you suspect any particular user of being responsible for massive disk usage; however, if you don't know where to start looking for the culprit, the "find" command may be more useful. This program is described more fully in chapter 5 , but notice now that between its options to find files by size, owner, and date, you have a powerful tool for discovering the disk-eater. For instance, the command

```
user      ->    find /usr -size +1000 -a -mtime -2 -a
          ->    -exec ls -l {}''{'';}
```

will run "ls -l" on all files in /usr larger than 1000 blocks that have been modified in the last two days. This might well tell you exactly why you ran out of space.

Find is also useful for building a list of files that have not been accessed for a given time (say, two months). Frequently if you bring such files to the attention of their owners, the owners will admit that the files can be deleted or archived to tape. This can save substantial amounts of disk space. (For archiving files to tape, see tar(Chapter 9.10).

9.4.2. Memory and Processes

It is possible for your system demands to increase to such an extent that you run into the limits on memory or on processes. These two problems are closely related in their symptoms; they appear as serious degradation of response time if they are of moderate seriousness, and can stop the system totally if things are severely wrong.

Reaching the limits of memory manifests itself as "thrashing", which is the operating system spending so much of its time giving people their turns at the CPU that the time-sharing routines actually take up more of the machine's time than the programs that the time-sharing is supposed to manage. If this happens frequently, you may need more memory. If, on the other hand, you suddenly experience a dramatic slowdown and suspect that somebody is just doing too much computing, you can use the "PS" command. You should be familiar with what the output from "ps" looks like when things are normal; if you run "ps" and find that somebody is running 10 "nroff" jobs at once, for instance, you may well want to advise them that this is hurting everybody's system performance.

Finally, you might actually run into the limit on processes. UNIX allows only a fixed number of processes to run at a time; this number is installation-dependent. If you do try and run too many processes at once, the system will simply refuse to create the new process. The shell indicates this refusal by typing "try again" if it does happen. In such a case you may be able to use "ps" to see if somebody has forked off many processes by accident. If all attempts to "ps" are met with "try again", about all you can do is get people who are in the editor to save their work and get everyone to logoff. This may reduce the number of processes running to the point where you can run "ps". If this does not help, you must crash (i.e., bring down ungracefully) the system by halting the CPU then rebook the system and fix any file systems that have been damaged as a result of the crash. Fortunately, it is rare that someone fills up the process table this badly by mistake.

If needed, you can reconfigure your kernel to increase the limit on the number of processes.

9.4.3. Accounting

There are two standard UNIX programs that will do accounting for you: "ac", which performs login accounting to see how much time each user uses, and "sa", which analyses a log of executions of shell commands.

The program itself just generates a human-readable summary of the login statistics; the actual logging is done by the routines invoked whenever a user logs in or out.

For this accounting to happen, the file /usr/adm/wtmp must exist; if it does not exist, no accounting takes place.

The command

/etc/accton /usr/adm/acct

in your /etc/rc file will enable this log-keeping.

Remember that both of the data files will tend to grow to excess and should be cleared regularly – perhaps once a month.

9.5. Some Odds and Ends

This chapter covers some miscellaneous pieces of system procedure: the file /etc/rc, which is run each time UNIX comes up multi-user; the program /etc/cron, which can be used to run programs automatically at a given time of each day, week or month; the file /etc/ttys, which tells UNIX what kind of terminals are attached where; how to unstick the line printer; and some words on shell files.

9.5.1. The File /etc/rc

The file /etc/rc is a shell file which is run automatically each time UNIX comes up multi-user. You should be aware of what it does so that you can modify it when necessary.

The /etc/rc file generally contains three types of commands. It will have "mount" commands, which are detailed elsewhere – they put your non-root file systems on the directory tree; it will have "housekeeping" commands – perhaps including something like "rm /tmp/*" to clear /tmp, or some local accounting procedures; and it will have lines that start up programs called "daemons". A daemon is a program that does not really belong to any user in many cases it executes as long as UNIX runs, checking every once in a while to see if it needs to do anything, for example, /etc/cron and /etc/update. The /etc/cron program is explained below the /etc/update program forces disk updates every thirty seconds and should be run at every installation.

9.5.2. The Program /etc/cron

The program /etc/cron is used to run other programs at regular time intervals. It reads from the input file /usr/lib/crontab, which has the format detailed in cron's entry in the manual. To give a quick example, suppose you have a procedure called "/usr/adm/dumper" which takes nightly tape dumps, and you want to have this run at 8:00 PM every weeknight. The requisite line in /usr/lib/crontab would be:

0 20 * * 1-5 /usr/adm/dumper

This line says that at minute 0, hour 20, every day of every month, but only on Monday through Friday: run /usr/adm/dumper.

Note that in order for the "cron" program to be running at all, it must be invoked somewhere. A good place to start /etc/cron is in /etc/rc.

9.5.3. The File /etc/ttys

This file contains information about each terminal.

Each line of the "ttys" file describes one port. The first character on each line is "0" or "1": "0" lines will be ignored. Next comes a character describing the terminal type. The code for this will be installation dependent, but "0" is always used for dial-in lines and the console. The remainder of the line is the name of the special file in /dev that refers to the port. For example, the line

10console

indicates that /dev/console is configured for login.

The actual physical ports are on the back of one of the mainframe cabinets. You might want to attach a little label to each outlet with the letter of its port so that you can move terminals from port to port.

9.5.4. The Line Printer Spooling Mechanism

If your installation has a line printer, the chances are that from time to time you will have trouble with its associated spooling mechanism. Here we explain how that mechanism works, and present procedures for clearing up problems that can arise. spooling is simply the means users can arrange to have files printed without having to worry about whether the printer happens to be available or not. (The term comes from "SPOOL", for Simultaneous Peripheral Operation On-Line).

Users spool files by using the "lpr" command. "lpr" places a copy of the file to be printed in the directory "/usr/lpd", along with a short file saying what to do with it and on whose behalf. Then "lpr" executes the line printer daemon "/etc/lpd".

"Lpd" first checks for the presence of a file named "lock" in the "/usr/lpd" directory. If it is there, "lpd" exits, assuming that another instance of itself is still active; otherwise, it creates the lock file. Thus, at most one instance of "lpd" can be active at once. Once the daemon has created the lock file, it keeps looking for command files, following their instructions, then removing them. When there are no more command files, the daemon removes its lock file and then exits.

On some systems the line printer occasionally gets "stuck". The symptoms of this are 1) nothing that is sent through "lpr" is printed; 2) the directory /usr/lpd has the files in it for printing; 3) the printer is on-line. To fix this problem do a "ps a". Look for a process that is called "lpd" or "/etc/lpd". Note the number of this process. Now issue "kill -3

PROCID" – PROCID being the "lpd" process number. This should start the printer.

If there is no "lpd" process, remove the lock file and try starting one up, thus:

```
user    ->    rm -f /usr/lpd/lock<r>
user    ->    /etc/lpd<r>
```

If this does not work, you may have some other problem. For a start, test the line printer by typing:

```
user    ->    echo stuff > /dev/lp<r>
```

The printer should print the word "stuff" and eject a page. If this still doesn't work, you may have hardware problems.

Sometimes, somebody will spool a file to the line printer with "lpr", and then decide that no printout of the file is wanted after all. To get rid of the unwanted file, first stop the printer by taking it ofline. Then "chdir" to "/usr/lpd" and do "ls -l". Note that "lpr" creates two files here each time it is run; a small file of commands for the line printer daemon named with "dfa" and a number, and a copy of the data to be printed on a file whose name ends in the same number. Try to guess, on the basis of file owner and size, which file is the one to be removed. "cat" one or more files (interrupting the output after the first few lines) if necessary to make sure; then remove the file and the corresponding "dfa" file.

If the unwanted file has already started to be printed, the above steps are still appropriate. Afterward, however, you must kill the line printer daemon, remove the lock files and start up another daemon, then put the printer back on-line.

This all sounds complicated, so let's go through a complete example. Suppose user Joe accidentally typed

```
user    ->    lpr <bigmodule.o<r>
```

when what was intended was:


```
user     ->    lpr <bigmodule.c<r>
```

Now, object code does not look pretty coming out on the printer, and it usually contains form feed characters, which cause the printer to throw out a lot of paper. On seeing this we stop the printer by hitting the OFFLINE button. We then go to our terminal, where we are already logged in, and the following session ensues:


```
user     ->    chdir /usr/lpd<r>
user     ->    ls -l<r>
UNIX  ->
```


```
total 6
-rw-rw-rw- 1 mary      226    Mar 17 03:28    cfa02324
-rw-rw-rw- 1 joe       843    Mar 17 03:25    cfa02326
-rw-rw-rw- 1 mary      63     Mar 17 03:28    dfa02324
-rw-rw-rw- 1 joe       63     Mar 17 03:25    dfa02326
-rw-rw-rw- 1 sue       41     Mar 17 12:29    dfa02329
– 1 daemon             0      Mar 17 12:14    lock
```


```
user     ->    rm [dc]fa02326<r>
user     ->    ps a<r>
UNIX  ->    8:  1356 - 0
```


```
->       2284    -
-> h:    393     - w
-> i:    2314    ed chapt.2
-> i:    12      -
-> 8:    2320    lpd
```

```
->      2337    ps a
->      2315    /bin/sh recompile
```

```
user   ->    kill 2320<r>
UNIX   ->    2320: not found
user   ->    su<r>
UNIX   ->    Password:
user   ->    <r>                    enter password, no echo
UNIX   ->    #                      superuser prompt
user   ->    kill 2320 <r>
UNIX   ->    #
user   ->    <r>                    cnt'l-d
UNIX   ->    $                      out of superuser
```

Between the '#\' and the '%' is a non printing character <CTRL>D.
Now we put the printer back on-line. It prints a little more garbage
(emptying the buffer), and ejects a final page. We rip off the paper, return
to the terminal, and type:

```
user   ->    rm -f lock<r>
user   ->    /etc/lpd<r>
UNIX   ->    $
```

and the printer starts on Mary's printout. End of example.

9.5.5. Useful Shell Files

One of the good things about UNIX is that it is very simple to make
up a "shell procedure" which contains commands to be executed. The
art of shell programming can produce highly sophisticated procedures that
are as complex as any program, but are also simple enough that a non-
programmer familiar with shell commands can put one together about as
fast as (s)he can type the commands themselves. Some places where shell

files would be appropriate are in a daily or weekly dump procedure, a daily housekeeping and/or accounting procedure, and in general any place where you have a standard list of commands to type. Shell files reduce the possibility of error; the more important and/or boring a procedure is, the better the idea of making it a shell procedure.

To make a shell procedure, simply edit a file and put in the commands that you want to run. You should include comments that explain what is going on. A comment can be entered by making the first character on a line a ':'; it must be followed by a space before the comment. (This is also the format for a label in a shell procedure.) When you are done editing the file, you must change the protection of the file so that the execute bit is on. A good protection for this is 775 "rwxrwxr-x", which lets everybody execute it and read it, while only you and members of your group can change it.

You may want to supply arguments to the procedure. In this case, you can use the shell variables $1,$2,$3...$9. The $1 variable is the first argument to the command, $2 the second, and so on. For instance, a simple procedure to list out and remove all of a directory might read:

```
user    ->    ls -l $1 > rmlist<r>
user    ->    rm $1/*<r>
```

If this file is called "cleanout", you can invoke it on /tmp by typing

```
user    ->    cleanout /tmp<r>
```

Finally, note that the command "shift" in a shell file bumps each argument up by one – $2 becomes $1, and so on. This allows you to make a shell procedure take an arbitrary number of arguments for processing; a version of "cleanout" that does this is:

echo >rmlist

for d do

ls -l $d >>rmlist

rm $d/*

done

You could now clean out several directories with one command line:

user   –>   cleanout direct1 direct2 direct3 <r>

9.6. File Systems: A Closer Look

At this point, we have referred to file systems many times. You have a vague idea of what they are and what they are for. You also know that a file system is a collection of files, and that a file system fits onto one disk (or else several fit on a larger disk); you know that file systems are attached somehow to the root directory tree; and you know that they must be guarded from damage lest damage beget damage. Now you will learn the secrets of the file systems.

9.6.1. Structure of any File System

Here is the overall picture of a file system. The parts are explained below.

block

0	boot block
1	superblock
2	
	i-list
2 + isize		(not to scale)
	data,
	indirect,
	and free
fsize	

UNIX views any disk (or part of a big disk) that can hold a file system as a sequence of blocks of 512 characters (or "bytes"). The blocks are generally thought of as being numbered 0, 1, 2,... on any given disk (or part). For each file system, there is:

1) a bootstrap block (block 0)

    – used during the booting of UNIX.

    It is not really involved in the file system format.

2) the "superblock"

    (block 1)

    – the "header data" for the file system. It includes the file system size ("fsize"), the number of blocks that can contain i-nodes ("isize"), and the head of the list of free blocks (we're simplifying a bit here; for the full-blown format see File System(V) or FILSYS(5) in the UPM).

3)   some blocks of i-nodes

(the "i-list")

– each file on the file system has exactly one i-node (there are 8 i-nodes to a block). The i-node contains information pertaining to the type of a file (regular, device, or directory); the owner of the file; the protection bits; the number of links to a file – remember that UNIX allows people to share files in this manner; the file size; the dates of most recent file access (reading) and modification (writing); and pointers to the actual data blocks of the file. The root directory of the file system is i-node 2.

4)   some blocks of data. The actual data in the files are contained here. Unused blocks in this part of the file system are chained to form the free list.

Also mixed with the data blocks are indirect blocks, which are blocks, i.e., full of block numbers. If a file is over a certain size, the i-node points to one or more indirect blocks, which in turn point to the actual data blocks. The i-node of an extremely large file could have 10 pointers to data blocks, a pointer to an indirect block that points to data blocks, a pointer to an indirect block that points to indirect blocks that point to data blocks, and a triple-indirect pointer.)

An i-number is the number of an i-node (the "i" stands for "index"), where the first i-node is numbered 1, the second 2, and so on. The i-number of a file may be thought of as the system's internal name or identifier for the file.

The i-nodes are allocated to files in the order that they become available. Since a typical UNIX installation has a lot of file creation and deletion going on, i-node numbers are pretty well scattered and unpredictable. The situation is the same for block numbers.

Closely related to the question of file systems is the format of a directory. Unlike many other systems, UNIX keeps only two pieces of information in a directory entry: the i-node number and the file name as it is known in that directory. This is how a file can have more than one link to it; two directories have entries with the same i-node number. It also makes clear that UNIX files do not have names intrinsically associated with them; the names are provided by the directory, not by the i-node. All other information is contained in the i-node. Thus when UNIX tries to open a given file name in your directory, it goes to the directory, finds the i-node number, then goes to that i-node in the file system; it then checks permissions from the i-node and finds the beginning of the data.

You should also be aware that UNIX considers devices – terminals, tape drives, disk drives, even main memory – to be "special files"; they thus have i-nodes. The file/device equivalence is deeply ingrained in UNIX; this is why a program can take input from either a file or a device, depending on what you tell the shell to have it do.

9.6.2. Mounted File Systems

A particular file system is identified in your kernel configuration as the root file system. The root file system contains the bare essentials that you need to run UNIX; when you bring up UNIX and are running as a single-user, you are running with just the root file system. What, then, of all the others that you have?

The other file systems sit on other disk drives and, until called upon, are basically unknown to UNIX. The way to make UNIX aware of a non-root file system is to "mount" the file system on the root. Suppose, for instance, you want to mount the file system on disk /dev/rp9. First you must have a place to mount it; this place is simply a directory. Assuming an empty directory named "/fs" had been created for mounting purposes, whenever you want to mount the file system on disk /dev/rp9, you could type:

user   -> /etc/mount /dev/rp9 /fs\<r>

From this mounting until /dev/rp9 is unmounted or the system goes down, the original directory /fs and anything below it is inaccessible. Any reference to /fs is now a reference to the top-level directory of the file system on /dev/rp9. If you were to mount /dev/rp9 instead on a file called /fstwo, a file (on the mounted system) that would have been called /fs/dir1/file1 would be called /fstwo/dir1/file1. In this way, the apparent size of the UNIX "file system" as the ordinary user perceives it is expanded far beyond the limits of an individual disk. Note that the opposite of "mount" is "umount" (not "unmount"); for example,

```
user    ->    /etc/umount /dev/rp9<r>
```

(Note that these two programs are in /etc, not in /bin.)

You will have a standard set of file systems to be mounted in standard places. The "mount" commands for these should be in /etc/rc, which you will recall is the shell file that is run when the system goes from single-user to multi-user. The particular file systems that you have will be installation-dependent; you will have exactly one root file system, and one or more user file systems. You may have an entire file system of scratch space (/tmp); if you do not you will just have a scratch directory /tmp on the root file system.

" Since /tmp tends to grow wildly (though it shrinks

about as fast), this isn't too good an idea"

The issue of which file systems go where and how large they are will be determined by you based on the available hardware and how you will be using the system.

9.7. Dumps

The most important responsibility of the system administrator is to take, or arrange for the taking of, regular tape dumps. This means that some or all of the files on the disk file systems are written out to a magnetic tape in such a way that they can be retrieved in the event that the files are deleted, either accidentally by the user, deliberately by a user who later changes his/her mind about the deletion and wants the file, or totally unpredictably by the system in the event of a system foul-up. (It is also possible for you, as the superuser, to make a mistake and delete somebody else's file. You, of course, will be very careful not to do this. After you have made your first embarrassing mistake and deleted somebody's important file, you will be even more careful in the future.) If for any of these reasons a file is deleted, and in addition you have no recent backup of the file, you will be sorry.

9.7.1. When to Take Dumps

The UNIX dump program, described below (and in more detail in Chapter 9.10), allows you to dump onto tape only those files that have been changed after a certain time, which you specify. If you specify the special time "zero", the complete file system is dumped.

The issue of when to take dumps, and how comprehensive each dump is to be, will depend on what your pattern of file activity is like. Suppose, for instance, that a full dump of your complete system takes up three 2400-foot tapes, and only a small proportion of your file system changes every day. You might want to take a weekly full dump and take "incremental dumps", as they are called, every night on a smaller tape. In this fashion you can get any day's complete system back by restoring only the full dump and the right day's incremental dump. If, on the other hand, you had one file system containing data that changed every day, you might want to take a daily full dump of that system only, and use the above scheme on the other file systems. You can determine a reasonable dump scheme when your system is installed, but you should know the rationale behind it so that you can adjust it if your pattern of file system use changes.

The question of how long to save the dumps must also be addressed. On the one hand, tapes cost money and you don't have an infinite number of them, so you will want to re-use them; on the other hand, the best dump procedure in the world is useless if the tapes have been written on since the dump you want was taken. One scheme that has proven effective is to save the daily, incremental dumps for a week after they are made; save the weekly dumps for about a month; and perhaps save the monthly tapes forever – that is, away from the machine, so that nobody will take them and overwrite them. This may seem excessive, but someday somebody is going to want something they deleted six months ago, and you will make them very happy by being able to give them some version of what they want.

9.7.2. How to Take Dumps

The UNIX dump/restore programs are described in full in section 9.10, but some of the more common modes of use are outlined here. You will probably want to write shell procedures to automate your dumping once you figure out just what it is that you want to do.

At this point we might mention that you should run file system integrity checks on your file systems before you take a dump. Dumps are supposed to be a safe backup; if the file system is damaged at the time you make the dump, the whole point of the operation is lost.

DEVICE is the name of the special file that represents the disk (or disk partition) containing the file system to be dumped. For example, /dev/rrk0 is the name for drive 0 of an RK05 disk subsystem. This dumps all ("a") files on the file system modified since "time zero" ("0") and updates ("u") the internal log to indicate that a full dump was taken at this time.

To take an incremental dump of the same file system, use:

```
user    ->    dump 9 /dev/rrk0
```

This dumps all the files (in the file system on disk rk0) that have been changed since the last full dump of that file system.

If at all practicable, dumps should be taken when there is little or no user activity on the system. This is to reduce the incidence of files being modified while they are being dumped. Such an event may sometimes be detected by the dump program and reported as a "phase error".

Incidentally, "dump" and "ncheck" do not require the file system they are working on to be mounted.

9.7.3. How to Restore Individual Files

A procedure will be given here that assumes that each dump is only one tape volume and that you are interested in just one file.

Mount the latest dump tape that may have a good version of the file you want. Do a command of the form:

```
user    ->    restor x FILE
```

– replacing FILE with the name of the desired file, stripped of any mount point name prefix. For example if the file is normally called

"/a/b/c" but "/a" is the name of the mount point, use "/b/c". In other words, file names on the tape are relative to the file system dumped.

If restor says the file is not there, presumably the tape you mounted is an incremental dump and you will have to go back to the full dump tape and start over. Otherwise, it will give you the file's i-number and type "mount the desired tape volume". The file will then be read from the tape and saved on a file in your current directory, and named with the original file's i-number in decimal. If you want the file saved under its old name, you will have to rename it.

9.7.4. Restoring an Entire File System

If a file system gets totally garbled, you may find that you want to restore the entire file system from tape. This is a last-ditch emergency measure, but here's how to do it. First, make sure the file system you are restoring onto is not mounted. If it is the root file system, the only way to do this is to bring the system down and bring up a backup copy of UNIX. Otherwise, type:

```
user    ->    /etc/umount DEVICE
```

If "umount" complains "mount device busy", someone is using it. That is, their current directory is on the file system in question, or they have some file on it open. Ask everyone to "chdir" to some other directory (including yourself!), then try the "umount" command again. Of course, you don't have to worry about unmounting non-root file systems if you are up in single-user mode, since it will not have been mounted. As soon as you succeed in getting the file system unmounted, do:

```
user    ->    /etc/mkfs DEVICE SIZE
```

– where DEVICE is whatever /dev name your disk is on, and SIZE is the size of the file system in blocks. This totally and irretrievably zaps the file system, so be sure you have done it right – in particular, make sure you have specified the right file system! In fact, it might be a good idea to dump the file system before swapping it.

Mount the full dump tape that you are restoring from and issue:

user   -> restor r DEVICE

If you want, you can then mount the latest incremental dump tape and do the "restor" procedure on that as well.

9.8. Repairing Damaged UNIX File Systems

Now that you know what a file system has inside it, you are ready to learn how to repair it when it gets damaged. The word "damaged" in this context refers to inconsistencies in the control information for the file system or bad data in the files; it rarely implies physical damage to the disk drives themselves. The art of fixing file systems depends on experience and confidence; it will take a while before you really feel comfortable, especially as you recall the consequences of certain errors. If you are going to repair a file system and think you may get it messed up – especially if there seems to be a lot of confusing damage – you might well want to dump it to tape beforehand.

Before starting to fix a file system, be sure none of your users can get at it. You want to be the only one doing anything to it. Usually, the best way to assure this is to have the system up single user.

9.8.1. The Basic Checking Programs

As mentioned earlier, the basic file integrity programs should be run 1) whenever the system is brought up; 2) when the system seems to have something mysterious wrong with it, and 3) daily, if at no other point. You should be aware that running the checks on "live" file systems while UNIX is running may give bogus error messages, since the disk may be in the process of being updated as the checks run. Even more important, the file system should be unmounted if possible when you are actually repairing damage, otherwise you are performing surgery on a patient while the patient is jogging.

There are two checking programs: "icheck" and "dcheck". The "icheck" program checks the consistency of the i-node structure and free-block list of the file system; the "dcheck" program checks the consistency of the directory structure. You will probably want to make up a shell procedure called something like "chk" to run these programs on your regular set of file systems. Also, notice that for every UNIX block device such as disks and tapes there is a "raw device"; that is, in addition to /dev/rk0 you have /dev/rrk0. This is the same as the regular device but the system can perform more eficient i/o on it. The "icheck" and "dcheck" programs can take these in place of the regular devices, and will run faster if you supply them instead.

Before we go much further, note this: we will be discussing ways of fixing file systems by changing data on the disk. After you think a file system has been fixed, run both "icheck" and "dcheck" again to be sure. The techniques presented in this chapter can sometimes have side effects that themselves must be taken care of. Hence, fixing file systems is an iterative process. As you become more experienced, you will learn to cut down the number of iterations. But it is still good practice to run the checking programs one final time to make sure, even if you think you have eliminated all the problems.

If you are repairing your root file system, you must HALT the machine and REBOOT the system immediately after you fix the errors because the system stores the root file system's control data in core as well as on disk, rewriting the information from core to the disk when forced to. Fixing file system errors only writes the corrected version on disk; if you let the system continue to run bad data will be rewritten out from core eventually and thereby invalidate your repair work. The basic complication of fixing the root file system is that it cannot be unmounted. The two possible solutions to this are to halt and reboot as outlined above, or to boot a backup system. If you are using the former method, having the system single-user is absolutely essential. Never add files to nor add to a file on a sick file system.

9.8.2. Icheck Output

The number of each block in the data blocks area of a healthy file system is either in the free list or in the list of blocks belonging to some file, but not both. Each block (number) must occur exactly once on exactly one of these lists. "Icheck" finds deviations from this rule. A block number occurring more than once is a duplicate. One occurring less than once is called missing. Of course, all the block numbers on the lists are supposed to be in the proper range (from 2 + isize up to but excluding fsize). "Icheck" detects violations of this, too. Out of range block numbers are called bad.

In an earlier section we showed the "normal" output of "icheck". Let's see it again, and explain it in more detail:

/dev/rp1:

files 540 (r=446,d=47,b=13,c=34)

used 8751 (i=212,ii=7,iii=0,d=8525)

free 6614

missing 0

The "files" name contains the total number of all kinds of files; "r" gives the number of "regular files"; "d" gives the number of directories; "b" gives the number of block special files; and "c" gives the number of character special files. "used" is total number of blocks in use and the numbers of single-, double-, and triple- indirect blocks and directory blocks. "free" is the number of blocks not being used right now.

1) Free-list errors: The free-list is a list of block numbers, each of which refers to a block that can be allocated by UNIX for use as a data block. If this gets messed up, it can be either harmless or horrible. If blocks are missing, then those blocks are not available for use. If there is one block missing, it's not harmful (though of course you lose one block); if there are hundreds, you have a problem. If, on the other hand, blocks on the free list should not be there, you have a potentially frightful situation; blocks that belong to a file may be allocated to a new file as well, causing all sorts of havoc.

There are three sorts of diagnostics from "icheck" pertaining to these cases:

missing #

#dup; inode=0, class=free

#dups in free

(The character '#' is replaced by the appropriate number in each case.) The first case corresponds to the relatively harmless case where there are missing blocks; the second two are potentially disastrous on an active file system. If any of these errors appear, ignore any others for the time being and perform the following fix:

user   ->   icheck -s /dev/???

The "-s" option stands for "salvage". It regenerates the free list to consist of all the blocks that are not in files.

If this is the root system, halt and reboot immediately after doing the salvage. Errors of the next type will be detected during the "icheck -s".

2) I-node errors: These are announced by the error messages:

b#bad; inode=i#; class=[iclass]

b#dup; inode=i#; class=[iclass]

In the above, [iclass] can be either: 1st, 2nd, or 3rd indirect, or data (small, large, huge, or "garg"). In each of these cases (bad or dup), you have to destroy the files involved (more on that below). In the "dup" case, you will not have been told all of the i-nodes involved since the duplication was only noted at the second occurrence of the indicated block in a file; the first occurrence must also be found in order for you to take care of it. To find all of the files associated with the dup'ed block, run:

user   ->   icheck -b #/dev/??? <r>

This will list all i-nodes associated with block '#'. All of these must be destroyed.

NOTE: If you have any of these messages with class= huge or gargantuan, you may also have any number of other, spurious error messages.

This is probably because you have a bad indirect block, which contains a whole lot of control information, all of which is totally wrong. If this happens, do not panic. Look through all of the error messages – there may be hundreds – and find the one that has a bad block in class=data(large). Destroy the file in the i-node given in that message. Now run "icheck" again on that file system. Most likely, all or most of the other errors will have gone away.

Because dups can be between the free list and files, if your initial "icheck" run shows any dups, try a salvage. If you are lucky, all the dups will go away. Otherwise, you will have to destroy files as described above.

All "icheck" detected errors should be cleared up before you go on to "dcheck".

9.8.3. Dcheck Output

Recall that every i-node contains a link count, which is supposed to be the number of directory entries that point to this i-node. Whenever the last link is removed, the kernel is supposed to actually delete the file, that is, free up all its blocks and mark its i-node as free, too. Hence, no files should have zero links. "Dcheck" detects violations of these rules.

In the case where there are no errors, "dcheck" will simply print the name of the device whose file system is being checked. If errors do exist, "dcheck" will list out a table with these columns:

inode	entries	linkcount
#	#	#
#	#	#

The inode is of course the i-node number. The "entries" is the number of directories that have that i-node listed as being a file in that directory. The linkcount is the number in the i-node itself, telling how many links the file thinks it has. Normally, "entries" and "linkcount" are equal and non-zero for each file; "dcheck" lists only those cases where they are unequal or both zero. Here is what to do in any of these cases:

1) entries=linkcount=0: The i-node is "allocated" but has no links. This

is not a dangerous situation, but it can be easily fixed by clearing the i-node. To do this do:

user   ->   clri /dev/???   inumber<r>

using the appropriate device name. You can also use the raw interface to the device, and you can clear any number of i-nodes by listing their numbers on one command, for example:

user   ->   clri /dev/rhp00 241 1001<r>

for each i-node that needs to be cleared, using the "cooked" interface to the device (for example, "clri 241 /dev/rk0", not "clri 241 /dev/rrk0"). After doing a series of "clri"s on a cooked device, type "sync". Use care to type the correct i-number.

2)   entries is less than linkcount: If entries=0, you can do a "clri" as in the above case on that i-node. If both numbers are greater than zero, the thing to do is bide your time; as links to that file are removed, both of the counts will drop until the entries=0. Then do the "clri".

3)   entries is greater than linkcount: This is very dangerous! The file has some links to it but the i-node itself thinks that there are fewer than there are. When links are removed, at some point the inode's linkcount will go to zero (causing the i-node to be reallocated) but some directories will still think that the file is theirs. Result: horrible havoc. You must destroy the file and remove all directory references to it. See "file destruction" below.

After fixing all the "dcheck" errors you are going to, go back to "icheck" to salvage the missing blocks that will have appeared as a result of your "clri"ing.

9.8.4. File Destruction

This section explains how to destroy files. Normally, files are removed by giving the "rm" command, but if there are any file system errors "rm" can cause more corruption of the system. In this section you are given a more surgical sort of technique, which involves zapping the i-node and removing any directory references to it. It is presumed that you know the i-node number; this can be gotten from the file name by doing an "ls -i" on the directory containing it. If the file you are required to destroy is a directory, don't rush ahead just yet; see the next section of this chapter.

Before you destroy a file, you might want to try and recover the contents of it. The name of the file can be gotten from the "-i" option of "ncheck"; this will give you an idea of how important the file is. The best way to salvage a file that is about to be destroyed is to do a simple "cp" of it to a different, healthy file system. Since creating new files on a corrupt file system can make the situation worse.

Of course, if the file in question contains dups or bads, the data you recover will be questionable. In the case of a block duplicated between two files, the chances are one will be correct and the other wrong.

In the case where you want to destroy a non-directory regular file, the procedure is:

1) Find the file name(s) under which the i-node is known, if you don't know already. To do this, do:

```
user    ->    ncheck -i [inode#] /dev/???<r>
```

You will get a list of file names associated with that file.

2) Mount the file system:

```
user    ->    /etc/mount /dev/???  filesystemname<r>
```

3) Copy any of the files you are going to use, to a healthy file system, or to tape.

4) Do "rm -f" on each name given by ncheck.

5) Unmount the file system.

6) Do a "clri" on each i-node involved on the file system.

7) Do "sync".

8) Again, "icheck -s" would also be a good idea. REMEMBER TO
    REBOOT IF IT'S THE ROOT FILE SYSTEM!!!

9.8.5. Destroying a Directory

You mustn't just zap the i-node of a directory, because then all of
the files under it in the directory structure are lost. Before you destroy
the directory, try and make a new directory somewhere in the file system,
and link to all of the members of the doomed directory. Then you can do
"rm" on all of the file names in the doomed directory. Now the directory
is empty, and can be zapped as in the last section (except that you must
use "rmdir" rather than "rm -f".

If you can't find the files in the doomed directory because the damage
is too great, you could zap the directory and run "dcheck" again; in this
case you will probably lose the files under the directory. You will appreciate
again the value of regular disk backups if this should happen to you.

9.9. Using a Back-up Copy of UNIX

It is a good idea to maintain a backup copy of the operating system for
dealing with situations where the normal root file system may be damaged.
If, for instance, you were to accidentally lose the shell or the "init" program, whether due to a mistyped command while in Superuser mode, or
due to hardware problems, you would be unable to use your main system
at all. In that case, having a backup system could save the time that would
otherwise be required to get a copy from another UNIX installation in order
to rebuild UNIX.

9.9.1. What Is A Back-up UNIX

A backup copy of UNIX (or simply "backup system") is a copy of your
root file system, kept on a disk or tape that is not normally mounted on
any drive on your computer.

If the backup system is away from the computer, then no error on your or the machine's part can hurt it.

It is most convenient to keep the backup system on a disk. However, if you have only one disk drive, a disk backup is not suficient for all eventualities, and you should have a backup system on tape. Using a backup system from tape resembles the process of installing UNIX for the first time on your computer.

9.9.2. Possible Differences in Configuration

It may be necessary to have one or more different kernel configurations, in addition to the one you normally boot, for emergency situations. If this is the case, a copy of each configuration should be kept on your normal root file system as well as on the backup system.

As an example, on our Computer (at the time of this writing), there are a big disk and four little disks. The normal kernel configuration we run (on a file with link "/unix") has its root and swap devices on the big disk. An alternate configuration ("rkunix") is set up with one of the small disks as its root and swap device. We can boot it in case the big disk is not working.

As another example, a site has two disk drives, each of which has a removable disk. Each disk holds 9000 blocks. The drives are equipped with switches that allow the unit numbers to be changed, so that it is possible to boot from either drive. Because of the needs of this site, the normal root file system takes up the entire 9000 blocks of a disk, so the swap space must be on the other disk. A different configuration, with a smaller root file system, is used for the backup disk. This backup system contains both its root file system and its swap area on the same disk. This alternate configuration is necessary so that the backup system will not use the main system for its swap area and thereby overwrite it.

9.9.3. Repairing Root File Systems

When there is only minor damage to your normal root file system, you can get away with repairing it without using the backup, as described in section 9.9.1. With the system up single-user, do any clri's that are indicated, then do "icheck -s", and halt and reboot the system without doing "sync" (which you otherwise always do before halting the processor). This is not as bad as doing surgery on a jogging patient; it is more like minor surgery performed on oneself.

However, when much repair must be done on the file system that is normally your root file system, it is better to bring up a backup system. Now, the file system that is normally the root system is no longer the root system (the backup is), and you can work on it, unmounted, like any other non-root file system.

Be sure to refer to the file system undergoing repair by the appropriate name while the backup system is up. For example, suppose you have two RK05 disk drives, and during normal operations /dev/rk0 is the root system and /dev/rk1 is mounted as /usr. Suppose you have decided to mount the backup system to repair the normal root file system. A reasonable way to proceed would be to (with the processor halted) replace the "/usr" disk with the backup disk, switch the drive unit numbers so that the drives exchange names, and boot the backup system. Then the disk that you normally call /dev/rk0 is now /dev/rk1.

The above remarks about working on the root file system also apply when you need to restore the root file system from a dump tape. To continue the example with the RK05's, you could restore the normal root system from the previous night's full dump tape by mounting the tape and typing the following commands to the backup system:

```
user   ->   /etc/mkfs /dev/rrk1 4000 <r>
user   ->   restor r /dev/rrk1 <r>
```

Last chance before scribbling on /dev/rrk1

```
user   ->   icheck /dev/rrk1 <r>
```

...

Once the normal root system is restored from the tape and appears healthy when ichecked and dchecked, you would type "sync", halt the processor, reload the disks that are normally loaded, switch the drive unit numbers back to normal, and boot the regular system.

9.9.4. Determining Whether a Problem is in Hardware or Software

Suppose you walk in one morning and your UNIX system is dead. Perhaps it typed a "panic" message on the console, or just halted the processor, or just won't take a login. The normal procedure would be to halt the processor (if it isn't already), reboot the system single-user, and start checking file systems. But suppose the system won't boot? In that case, the thing to do is try booting the backup system. If it doesn't work, the chances are you have a hardware problem and you would be justified in calling in a hardware repairer.

If, on the other hand, the backup system does boot, you should check the regular root file system with icheck and dcheck. After clearing up the problems indicated, make sure that the files /etc/init and /bin/sh match those on the backup system. For example, if your normal root file system is called "rk1" from the point of view of the backup system, the following could happen (after the icheck and dcheck gave a clean bill of health):

```
user   ->   /etc/mount /dev/rk1 /mnt<r>
user   ->   cmp /mnt/etc/init /etc/init <r>
user   ->   cmp /mnt/bin/sh /bin/sh <r>
UNIX   ->   /mnt/bin/sh /bin/sh differ: char 22 line 2
user   ->   cp /bin/sh /mnt/bin/sh<r>
user   ->   sync<r>
```

In this example, "init" appeared okay, but the shell appeared to have been garbaged. The system administrator then copied the shell on the backup disk ("/bin/sh") into the one on the normal root disk ("/mnt/bin/sh").

9.9.5. Questions

(1) Who are privileged users and what are their powers?

(2) Describe a procedure to add new users to the system.

(3) Before stopping the system how do you inform all active users?

(4) How do you check for active processes (both user and system processes)?

(5) When is a file system most likely to go bad?

(6) How can you see how much space is left on any file system?

(7) How can you automatically initiate special procedures when the system is brought up multi user?

(8) How do you activate or de-activate a terminal port?

(9) What is an i-number?

(10) What is a recommended way of taking tape dumps?

(11) How do you restore files from a dump?

(12) What are the two types of errors reported when running icheck?

(13) What is a recommended procedure for running checks on the file system?

9.10. Backup and Maintenance Commands

Maintenance of the system is one of the most important functions, because without it little or nothing would get done. Chapter 9 describes the duties of the system administrator and the responsibilities required of that job. However without the proper tools to help in the day to day activities of maintenance, it would be very dificult to accomplish this. Thus the UNIX system provides tools that help to provide such things as bringing the system up and down, adding and deleting users, taking tape dumps, recovering from unforeseen disasters, etc. Although chapter 9 describes the functions (combination of tools) necessary to perform these tasks, this section provides a little more detail on each of them.

The maintenance of UNIX is described in chapter 9 and includes the use of most of the commands defined in this section. In fact it tries to tie them together in a useful manner. It may be more advantagous to first read chapter 9 and then reference this section when you feel that more information is needed about an individual command.

The following commands are used by the system administrator when dealing with system maintenance.

9.10.1. File System Directory Consistency Check

Command: dcheck

Syntax: dcheck [-i numbers] [filesystem]

Function: This command is used to compare the link-count in each i-node with the number of directory entries by which it is referenced. It can also provide the name of entries specified by an i-number. Again this command is used during system administration (chapter 9 should be referenced before using it).

Option: no options are available with this command.

Example:

(1) The dcheck is run by the system administrator when checking the
     integrity of the file system. Section 9.8.3 provides more detail
     about the order in which these checks are made. The following is
     an example of what the output looks like when correct and when
     there are errors.

       user $->$ dcheck /dev/rp1 $<$r$>$
       UNIX $->$ /dev/rp1:

       entries   link   cnt
       $->$ 448   0   0
       $->$ 450   0   0
       $->$ 653   0   0
       $->$ 733   0   0
       $->$ 1317   0   0

     In this example all of the entries equal the link count which equals
zero. This indicates that the i-node is "allocated", but has no links. This
is not dangerous, but it can be easily fixed by clearing the i-node using the
command "clri".

       user $->$ dcheck /dev/rp1$<$r$>$
       UNIX $->$ /dev/rp1:

       $->$entries   link   cnt
       $->$ 6   2   4
       $->$ 39   1   0
       $->$ 40   1   0
       $->$ 46   0   0

```
-> 48      0      0
-> 51      0      0
-> 64      3      2
```

In this example, Inodes 39 and 40 are directory links pointing to nothing. Inode 64 still contains data (of questionable validity). All references to these inodes must be removed, but first try to save any data in the files.

Summary:

Every i-node contains a link count, which is supposed to be the number of directory entries that point to a specific i-node. Once the file is free, all its blocks and its i-node is freed too. Thus no file should ever have zero links. This is the task of "dcheck", to detect violations of these rules.

If the dcheck finds no errors, it returns to UNIX with no message.

9.10.2. File System Storage Consistency Check

Command: icheck

Syntax: icheck [-s] [-b numbers] [filesystem]

Function: This command examines a file system. It checks for consistency for both the free block list and for the used blocks. The number of each block in the data blocks area of a healthy file system is either in the free list or in the list of blocks belonging to some file, but not both. Each block (number) must occur only once on exactly one of these lists.

A block number occurring more than once is a duplicate. One occurring less than once is called missing. Out of range block numbers are called bad. The normal output produced by this command is:

o   The total number of files and the number of
                           regular, directory, block special and character spe-
                           cial files.

o   The total number of blocks in use and the numbers
                           of single-, double-, and triple- indirect blocks and
                           directory blocks.

o   The number of free blocks.

o   The number of blocks missing (not found in any
                           file or in the free list).

Option: Two options exist for this command. They are:

-s   This option causes icheck to ignore the actual free
                           list and reconstruct a new one. The file system
                           should be dismounted while this is done. Once
                           the command has completed the system should
                           be rebooted. This is to assure that the new file
                           structure is placed on disk. You should not "sync"
                           before stopping the system for reboot. This op-
                           tion causes the normal output reports to be sup-
                           pressed.

-b   This option followed by a list of block numbers
                           will cause the command to produce a diagnostic
                           whenever the listed block number is found.

Example:

(1) Let's first look at an icheck that contains no bad data.

    user   ->   icheck /dev/rp1 <r>

```
UNIX ->    /dev/rp1:
     ->    files      739  (r=619,d=73,b=13,c=34)
     ->    used     11571  (i=277,ii=10,iii=0,d=11274)
     ->    free     3797
     ->    missing    0
```

This output can be interpreted as:

files: Contains the total number of all kinds of files. "r"
                          provides the number of regular files, "d" provides
                          the number of directories, "b" provides the number
                          of block special files, and "c" provides the number
                          of characters special files.

```
user  ->   icheck /dev/rp1<r>
UNIX  ->   /dev/rp1:
      ->   files      739  (r=619,d=73,b=13,c=34)
      ->   used     11571  (i=277,ii=10,iii=0,d=11274)
      ->   free     3
      ->   missing    3794
```

This example shows us that there are blocks missing from the free list. This is one of the more frequent errors and can be easily fixed by running the "icheck" command with the "-s" option, then rebooting the system without having "sync'd". If you leave it this way you will not be able to run because of the unavailability of free blocks.

Summary:

The important function of icheck is to insure the integrity of your file system, because without a clean file system you stand a good chance of losing much of your data. We have shown one example of a bad file system "Free-list errors". However there are other more critical errors which can occur. These errors will exist when there are blocks on the free list which should not be there. In this case you have a potentially frightful situation. Chapter 9 provides you with details on handling this type of problem.

9.10.3. Generate Names from i-numbers

Command:	ncheck
Syntax:	ncheck [-i numbers] [-a] [-s] [filesystem]
Function:	This command is used to produce pathnames vs. i-number list of all files on a specific file system. It's principal use is to locate names of files that may be improperly set in the file system.
Option:	The following options can be used with this

-i	produces a list of pathnames for the i-numbers that follow this option.
-a	produces the same list as with the "-i" option with the exception that files starting with "." and ".." which are normally suppressed will be printed.
-s	This option reduces the report to include only special files and files with set-user-ID mode. This can be used to discover concealed violations of security policy.

Example:

(1) From the resulting run of the command "dcheck", we found that the i-node numbers 39, 40 and 64 had problems. To find out what directories or files are referenced by these numbers we can simply run the "ncheck" command as follows:

```
user   ->   ncheck -39 40 64 /dev/rp1<r>
UNIX   ->   /dev/rp1:
```

```
->    64    /xxx3
->    40    /dq/trb/x
->    39    /dq/trb/x2
->    64    /working/xxx1
->    64    /working/xxx2
```

From this information we can then procede to investigate these specific files or directories and see if we can save them either by clearing the bad i-nodes, or making copies and then clearing.

Summary:

This command is generally used when you want to destroy a non-directory regular file and to do this you need to know the name of the file. As you can see from the example, the names of the files are produced based on the i-node numbers provided. Chapter 9 provides more detail on how this command is used in conjunction with other commands.

9.10.4. Clear i-nodes

Command:	clri
Syntax:	clri filesystem i-number. . .
Function:	The primary purpose of this command is to remove a file which for some reason appears in no directory. However there are also times when an i-node must be removed when it does appear in a directory. In this case care should be taken to track down the entry and remove it with a "rm" command before clearing the i-node. Before using this command read chapter 9, Administration of a UNIX system.
Option:	No options exist for this command.

Example:

(1) We must know the file system that we are in before we can delete
     any i-nodes. Once we have that information we must find out more
     about each i-node number before we delete them. The commands
     "dcheck,icheck,and ncheck" provide use with this information. Once
     we have determined that the i-node number is to be deleted we can do
     so by saying:

```
user   ->   clri /dev/rmt1 39 40 64<r>
UNIX  ->   #
```

Once you have cleared the i-nodes, you should perform a "sync" operation. It is usually a good idea to perform a "icheck -s" as well. Remember
that if you are in the root file system, you must reboot.

Summary:

Some of the reasons for clearing i-nodes are (1) entries=linkcount=0,
(2) entries are less than linkcount, (3) entries are greater than linkcount.
You must be aware of the dangers when clearing i-nodes. It is possible
to create more problems by clearing i-nodes than not, or at least without
carefully checking out all alternatives and trying to save the files before
clearing. Again as with other commands in this section, refer to chapter 9
for details on using clri.

9.10.5. Construct a File System

Command:	mkfs
Syntax:	/etc/mkfs [filesytem] [block count]
Function:	This command creates a new file system on a disk or part of a disk based on the number of blocks provided in the argument [block count]. This file system can then be used by attaching it to the root file system though the use of the mount command. This command destroys anything that was previously there. If, for example, an existing file system was in such bad shape that it could not be fixed, or that it would be too much effort to fix, then creating a new file system will destroy the contents of the current file system leaving you with an empty file system. This commmand must be issued before you start using any file system.
	Any new disk that is attached to your system must have this file system generated. Also notice that this command is not directly executable from the normal /bin or /usr/bin directories. This is because it is a special command that is controlled by the system administrator who will decide when a file system should or should not be built. Generally the directory "/etc" has read/write permission for the superuser only.
Option:	No options exist for this command.

Example:

(1) Create a file system on a new disk that's 15000 blocks. You must first find out what the file system has been called (if anything) by looking in the directory "/dev". If the file system name does not exist, you can create its name and characteristics by using the command "mknod"

or directly with this command and a special protocol(see UNIX programmers manual "mkfs(1m)").

In this case we will assume that the file system name exists. We can then create the new file system by entering:

```
user    ->    /etc/mkfs /dev/rp3 15000<r>
UNIX    ->    $
```

Summary:

As we stated before, if the file system name already exists in the directory "/dev", we can use this simple format as shown in the previous example. However if the name does not exist, you will have to provide a lot more information either directly through the mkfs command or using other commands in addition to the mkfs command.

9.10.6. Build Special Files

Command:	mknod
Syntax:	/etc/mknod name [c] [b] major minor
Function:	This command is used to make special files (see chapter 9 on system administration). Generally these special files are contained in the directory "/dev" which describes the characteristics of such things as device drivers (disk,tape,etc.) and the file systems available on this specific system. The major and minor device numbers generally pertain to a driver (major - for example the tty driver) and the specific entries in that driver (minor - each tty in the tty driver). These numbers are specific to each system and if not documented can be found in the system program source file named "conf.c".

As with several of the other commands, this
command has to be executed from the directory
"/etc". This is because it is a system command
used in the creation of special system functions.

Option: The two options specify that the special file is "b" -
block-type (disk,tape) or "c" - character-type (tty).

Example:

(1) Let's say we want to create a new name for an existing tty device. We
can first find the major/minor numbers of that device by issuing the
command "ls -l /dev" which will provide us with a list of all the special
files and their major/minor device numbers as well as their name and
if they are a character or block device. They will look as follows:

```
total 1
crw-w-w-      1 bin 0,     0    Jan 20 17:40    console
c-w-w-w-      1 bin 0,    40    Jan 20 17:38    lp
brw-rw-rw-    1 bin 1,     0    Jan 15 16:40    mt0
crw-rw-rw-    1 bin 3,     0    Jan 20 17:26    rmt0
brw r         1 bin 0,     1    Jan 16 18:01    rp1
brw-r-        1 bin 0,     2    Oct 29 04:07    rp2
brw-r-        1 bin 0,     3    Dec 16 10:40    rp3
crw-r-        1 bin 2,     1    Jan 16 18:03    rrp1
crw-r-        1 bin 2,     2    Oct 29 04:07    rrp2
crw-r-        1 bin 2,     3    Oct 29 04:07    rrp3
crw-w-w-      1 bin 0,     2    Jan 20 17:02    tty1
crw-w-w-      1 bin 0,     6    Jan 21 07:18    tty2
crw-w-w-      1 bin 0,     1    Jan 20 17:02    tty3
```

We can see that the first character of each entry provides us with the
type of entry (block or character), then the major/minor device number(i.e.,
0, 1), and last of all the name of the special file. The other information is
the same as that found in any "ls -l" command.

If we are to create a new entry (name) with the same characteristics
as an existing entry we can do so by entering:

```
user   ->    /etc/mknod ttyob c 0 1<r>
UNIX  ->    $
```

We can then see what we have created by entering the command "ls - 1/dev".

```
total 1
crw-w-w-   1 bin 0,    0    Jan 20 17:40    console
c-w-w-w-   1 bin 0,   40    Jan 20 17:38    lp
brw-rw-rw- 1 bin 1,    0    Jan 15 16:40    mt0
crw-rw-rw- 1 bin 3,    0    Jan 20 17:26    rmt0
brw-r-     1 bin 0,    1    Jan 16 18:01    rp1
brw-r-     1 bin 0,    2    Oct 29 04:07    rp2
brw-r-     1 bin 0,    3    Dec 16 10:40    rp3
crw-r-     1 bin 2,    1    Jan 16 18:03    rrp1
crw-r-     1 bin 2,    2    Oct 29 04:07    rrp2
crw-r-     1 bin 2,    3    Oct 29 04:07    rrp3
crw-w-w-   1 bin 0,    1    Jan 21 14:34    tty0b
crw-w-w-   1 bin 0,    2    Jan 20 17:02    tty1
crw-w-w-   1 bin 0,    6    Jan 21 07:18    tty2
crw-w-w-   1 bin 0,    1    Jan 20 17:02    tty3
```

We have now created a new entry "tty0b" which has the same characteristics as does the entry "tty3". If we want to create an entry that is different than any of the existing entries, we will have to understand the limitations of the special file we are creating. Again this information can be obtained from the system programs source file "conf.c".

Summary:

This command is directly tied into the system drivers and it is essential that you know more about the internals of the system than what is explained in this book. The kernal of UNIX is only about 10,000 source statements of which 800 or so are assembly and the rest are C language statements.

9.10.7. Mount a File System

Command:	mount
Syntax:	/etc/mount [file system [-r]]
Function:	The only file system that is automatically mounted when the system is booted is the "root file system". This file system contains the bare essentials that you need to run UNIX.
	All other file systems (see the command "mkfs") are unknown to UNIX until you execute the "mount" command. This can be done by you issuing the specific command, or automatically by the system when it is booted (see special files "/etc/rc" as defined in chapter 9). Once the file system has been mounted, it will remain mounted until you bring the system down or unmount it.
Option:	Only one option exists for this command "-r" and it specifies that the file system should be mounted as read only.

Example:

(1) Mount the file system whose name is rp3.

```
user   ->   /etc/mount /dev/rp3 programs<r>
UNIX  ->    $
```

The file system "rp3" has been defined in the directory "/dev" which defines the special files(i.e.,device drivers,etc.). It must exist or you will get an error message from the system. The named programs must be directories having already been created. Once this command has been executed the file system "rp3" will be made available through the root directory to the directory "programs".

Summary:

If you forgot to mount the file system "pr3" and try to access the data in that file system you will find that it is treating the directory "programs" as just another directory under the root file system. In addition the directory that is the root for each file system must be created in the UNIX root file system.

9.10.8. Dismount a File System

Command:	umount
Syntax:	/etc/umount file system
Function:	This command simply dismounts the specified file system if it is mounted. If it is not mounted a message to that effect will be given.
Option:	No options exist for this command.

Example:

(1) We will dismount the file system "rp3" which we just mounted in the previous example.

```
user   ->   /etc/umount /dev/rp3<r>
UNIX   ->   $
```

Summary:

This command would generally be controlled by the system administrator. As with some of the other special commands, it is found in the directory "/etc" and must be executed from there.

9.10.9. Substitute user ID Temporarily

Command:	su
Syntax:	su [userid]
Function:	This command allows you to change to another user's ID and perform tasks that may have been read/write protected if the tasks were performed from within your own userid. Your current directory and user environment is unchanged. If the userid you are changing to has a password, the system will request that you enter it. To return to your own environment you must strike the control key and the letter "d" at the same time "cntl-d". This will place you back in your own enviornment exactly as you were when you left. You will not be able to get into the new environment without it.
Option:	No options are available for this command.

Example:

(1) The most common use of this command is to become the superuser when you need to access directories or files and do not have permission under your current login name. To change to superuser you say:

```
user   ->   su<r>
UNIX   ->   Password:
user   ->   <r>            enter password,but not echo'd
UNIX   ->   #
```

You can tell that you are the superuser by the fact that the prompt "#" appears. If it had not allowed you to become superuser, it would have issued the prompt "$" instead.

(2) We can also enter as another user by issuing the login name of that
     user. Thus we say:

```
user   ->    su joe<r>
UNIX   ->    Password:
user   ->    <r>                    enter password,but not echo'd
UNIX   ->    $
```

You will now be in the directory of the other user and under control
of his permissions.

Summary:

This command is useful when you must have access to something that
you would otherwise not have permission to see. Again your original directory and environment is not changed when you return (return by striking
"cnt'l-d").

9.10.10. Update the Super Block

Command:	sync
Syntax:	sync
Function:	The UNIX system provides all users with buffers for controlling input/output. However as files are changed, deleted, or added, they are written onto the disk only every so often. Thus if at any time the system goes down (i.e., power failure, disk failure, etc.) the file system is subject to the status at that time. It can mean that your file systems could be destroyed or at least damaged. The "sync" command is used to flush out the buffers and update the file system on disk. It is automatically executed by the system every so often (execution is controlled by the system administrator, but generally updated between 30 seconds and two minutes). Each time the system is stopped the operator should perform a "sync" to insure that the disk copy reflects what is in memory.
Option:	No options exist for this command.

Example:

(1) Before stopping the system you should perform a "sync".

```
user   ->    sync<r>
UNIX   ->    $
```

Summary:

The only indication that the sync has performed its task is the UNIX prompt. If you are close to the computer, you may hear the disk move.

Once the system has gone down (power failure, etc.) it is too late to perform a sync. You will then have to check the file system using the other commands previously described (icheck, dcheck, etc.).

9.10.11. Tape Archiver

Command: tar

Syntax: tar [option] [name]

Function: This command saves and restores files on magtape. The exact function performed by this command is determined by the option or options specified. You have the ability to save and restore individual files or complete directories.

Option: The options are divided into two parts. The first is the specification of the function to be performed, and the second includes modifiers that may be added to a given function.

The following options specify the functions available:

r   The named files are written on the end of the tape.

x   The named files are extracted from the tape. If a complete directory and its files and subdirectories are written on the tape, then "x" will extract everything including the directories. If multiple entries of the same thing are on the tape, the last one will overwrite the previous one.

t

This function provides a listing of the files and directories on the tape based on the names provided. If no names are provided everything on the tape is listed.

u

The named files are added to the tape if they are not already there, or if they have been modified since the last time they were created.

The following options are used as modifiers to the functions specified above:

0,...,7

This modifier selects the drive on which the tape is mounted. The default is 1.

v

This option causes tar to print the name of each file or directory that has been affected by the function specified. Used with the "t" option, it provides more information than just the name.

w

this option causes tar to print the action to be taken followed by the file name, then wait for user confirmation. If you respond with a "y", the action is taken, otherwise any other character entered will cause the action to not be taken.

f

causes tar to use the next argument as the name of the archive instead of the tape "/dev/mt?". If the name of the file is "-", tar writes to the standard output or reads from the standard input. Thus it can be used in a filter chain.

b

used as the blocking factor when reading or writing files. The default is 1 and the maximum is 20.

l

this option is used to complain if all of the links to the files that are being dumped are not resolved.

m

this option tells tar not to restore the modification times. The mod time will remain that of the time when the files were extracted.

Example:

(1) First let's try to create a tape archive of the files in a single directory. We must position ourselves to the dirctory that contains the informa- tion that is being archived, or we must provide the complete path name.

```
user   ->   tar c0 directory1<r>
UNIX   ->   $
```

This command will write all of the files (and subdirectories) to the tape. All previous data on the tape will be destroyed. If we want to see what is being placed on the tape, we can use the option "v". Thus we would say:

```
user   ->   tar cv0 work<r>
UNIX   ->   a work/file1, 1 block
       ->   a work/file2, 3 blocks
       ->   a work/file3, 14 blocks
       ->   a work/file4, 2 blocks
       ->   $
```

In this example the only difference is that we have requested that the names of the files we are archiving on the tape be printed. The "a" indicates that the file is being added to the tape, and the block indicates the number of tape blocks that are required to hold it. As we pointed out before, this option "c" creates a new tape destroying everything that was previously on it. If we wanted to add new files to the tape or replace existing ones, we would use the option "r" instead of "c". Thus if the file did not exist, it would be added and if it existed, it would be replaced.

(2) Now let's see how the files can be blocked. This is generally necessary when you have large amounts of data to archive. The blocking allows more data to be placed on the tape than it would otherwise allow (because of the record gaps that are generated).

```
user   ->   tar cv0b16 work<r>
```

```
UNIX  ->    a work/file1, 1 block
      ->    a work/file2, 3 blocks
      ->    a work/file3, 14 blocks
      ->    a work/file4, 2 blocks
      ->    $
```

In appearance there is no difference; however, the amount of data that can be placed on the tape is much more than if no blocking were used. If you try without blocking and run out of tape, a message will be issued. In this case you will want to try again with the blocking being used.

(3) Any time that we would like to see what we have on any given tape, we need only use the option "t". This will allow us to see the contents of a tape before doing anything else.

```
user  ->    tar t0 work<r>
UNIX  ->    work/file1
      ->    work/file2
      ->    work/file3
      ->    work/file4
      ->    $
```

We are provided with only the names of the files, the byte count and block sizes are not provided.

(4) Now let's extract the files we have just placed on the tape. To accomplish this we will use the extract option "x". We must be positioned at the directory where we want the files to be placed.

```
user  ->    tar xv0 work<r>
UNIX  ->    x work/file1, 83 bytes, 1 block
      ->    x work/file2, 34 bytes, 3 blocks
      ->    x work/file3, 122 bytes, 14 blocks
      ->    x work/file4, 40 bytes, 2 blocks
      ->    $
```

In this case we are given the size of each file in bytes in addition to the number of blocks. The "x" indicates that the files are being extracted.

(5) Now that we have learned to create and extract files, let's see how we
     can use it as the front or rear end of a filter chain. In this case we will
     use the "dd" command to convert each file to ASCII from EBCDIC,
     first before writing to the tape and then after reading it from the tape.

```
user   ->   tar cvf - file1 | dd of=/dev/rmt0 conv=ascii<r>
UNIX   ->   a file1, 1 block
       ->   $
```

In this example, we are telling tar to create a new archive containing
the file "file1" and that before placing it on tape, we want to convert the
contents (which is EBCDIC) to ASCII. Now if we want to reverse this procedure and read the file from tape, converting it back to EBCDIC, we can
do so by saying:

```
user   ->   dd if=/dev/rmt0 conv=ebcdic | tar xvf - file1<r>
UNIX   ->   x file1, 1 block
       ->   $
```

The "dd" command is explained in chapter 7.2.2. Notice that when
we use tar in a filter chain, we must specify raw magnetic tape archive
"/dev/rmt0" is the raw I/O driver for mt0. Your raw I/O names can be
obtained from the directory "/dev".

Summary:

This command is useful to everyone and can be used for your own
personal backup tape.

9.10.12. Incremental File System Dump

Command: dump

Syntax: dump [option [argument...] filesystem]

Function: This command is generally used by the system
                            administrator for providing a back up of all the
                            data on the file systems. It provides the facility to
                            dump files based on various criteria such as dump-
                            ing only files that have changed for the day,etc.
                            Thus the system administrator can minimize the
                            amount of time that is required for taking dumps
                            by not having to create a complete dump each
                            day. Methods for taking dumps are explained in
                            chapter 9.

Option: The following options are used in conducting
                            dumps.

f   place the dump on the next argument file instead
                            of on the tape.

u   if the dump completes succcaofully, write the
                            date of the beginning of the dump on the file
                            "/etc/ddate". This file records a separate date for
                            each filesystem and each dump level.

0-9   this number is the "dump level". All files modified
                            since the last date stored in the file "/etc/ddate"
                            for the same file system at lesser levels will be
                            dumped. If no date is determined by the level, the
                            beginning of time is assumed. Thus the option 0
                            causes the entire file system to be dumped.

s   this option allows you to specify the size of the
                            dump tape(in feet). Immediately following the "s"
                            option is the numeric value specifying the size of
                            the dump tape. When the size specified is reached
                            during a dump, the dump will wait for the reel to
                            be changed. The default size is 2300 feet.

d   this option allows you to specify the density of
                           the tape, expressed in BPI. The argument follow-
                           ing this option is the numeric value of the density
                           "BPI". This is used to calculate the amount of
                           tape used per write. The default is 1600.

Example:

(1) To take an incremental dump of a file system, you can say:

```
user   ->    dump 9 /dev/rmt1<r>
UNIX  ->    #
```

This command will dump all the files (in the file system on disk rmt1)
that have been changed since the last full dump of that file system.

Summary:

Although this command is explained in more detail in chapter 9, it is a
necessary command for the system administrator. Too often this command
is not used on a consistent bases and will only be noticed the first time the
disk fails and all the data files are destroyed. Don't let that happen.

9.10.13. Incremental File System Restore

Command: restor

Syntax: option [argument...]

Function: This command is used to read magtapes that have
                    been dumped using the "dump" command.

Option: The following options can be used with this com-
                    mand.

f	this option allows you to use a specific tape instead of the default. The name of the tape is an argument which follows the "f" option.
r or R	This option allows you to specify the filesytem where the tape is read and loaded. The name of the filesystem is the argument following the the option "r or R". If the option is "R" instead of "r", restor asks which tape of a multi volume set to start on. This allows restor to be interrupted and then restarted (an icheck -s must be done before).
x	Each file on the tape named by an argument is extracted. The file name has all "mount" prefixes removed (i.e., /usr/bin/lpr is named /bin/lpr on the tape). Chapter 9 explains procedures for keeping the amount of tape read to a minimum.
t	this option prints the date the tape was written and the date the file system was dumped from.

Example:

(1) Normally you will want to restore specific files that have been damaged for whatever reason. To accomplish this you need only enter:

```
user   ->   restor x file1<r>
UNIX  ->   #
```

Remember to provide the file name or names stripped of any mount point name prefix. For example if the file is normally called "/user/dick/file1", but "/user" is the name of the mount point, use "/dick/file1". In other words, file names on the tape are relative to the file system dumped.

Summary:

This command is used with the "dump" command and is usually under the control of the system administrator. If, during a restore you find that the system cannot find a file, then presumably the tape you mounted is an incremental dump and you will have to go back to the full dump tape and start over. Restoring the entire file system from tape should always be a last-ditch emergency measure. See chapter 9 for details on restoring file systems.

9.10.14. Questions

(1) What are the purposes of the following commands?

  a) icheck

  b) ncheck

  c) clri

(2) Why must one use the "mount" command?

(3) If you find a file that has read/write permissions set such that you can't access it, what must you do to access it?

(4) When would you select the dump command over the tar command?

APPENDIX A

The UNIX kernel will print error messages on the system console in case of I/O device errors, overflowing of system tables, or errors in the operating system. This is a summary of those error messages.

err on dev d/d

bn ddddd er dddddd dddddd

This is a message printed in case of I/O device error. d/d is the major and minor device number of the device on which the error occurred. A list of major/minor device numbers and the devices they correspond to may be made with the following command:

```
user   ->   ls -l /dev | grep ''^b'' <r>
```

This will produce an output in a form like this:

brw-r–	1 bin	8, 0	Mar 13 15:13	hk00
brw-r–r–	1 bin	8, 1	Mar 27 12:06	hk01
brw-r–	1 bin	8, 2	Jan 13 14:32	hk02
brw-r–	1 bin	8, 3	Jan 13 14:32	hk03
brw-r–	1 bin	8, 4	Mar 13 15:18	hk04
brw-r–	1 bin	8, 8	Jan 13 14:32	hk10
brw-r–	1 bin	8, 9	Mar 10 09:30	hk11
brw-r–	1 bin	8, 10	Jan 13 14:32	hk12
brw-r–	1 bin	8, 11	Mar 13 23:22	hk13
brw-r–	1 bin	8, 12	Mar 10 16:53	hk14
brw-rw-rw-	1 bin	3, 0	Apr 10 17:45	mt0
brw-rw-rw-	1 bin	3, 4	Apr 10 01:27	mt4
brw-rw-rw-	1 bin	3, 32	Feb 12 21:44	nmt0
brw-rw-rw-	1 bin	3, 36	Aug 27 12:04	nmt4

This is a listing of the "block special files" in the "/dev" directory; this directory contains all the "special files" that refer to devices on the system. "Block special files" are the disk and tape devices.

The first three columns are not really different from those in a "ls -l" of ordinary files, except for the "b" at the beginning indicating a "block special file"; what is different is the next column, which is the file size in bytes for ordinary files. In the case of special files, this column contains the major and minor device number of that device, separated by a comma. Thus, the error message

err on dev 8/0

bn ddddd er dddddd dddddd

indicates an error on device "/dev/hk00", which in this case is the first part of RK07 drive 0.

ddddd after "bn" is the block number on the device where the error occurred. The numbers after "er" are two device error registers; which registers they are and what their contents mean is dependent on the kind of device on which the error occurred.

bad block on d/d

This is an error message printed in case of a corrupt file system. d/d again indicates the major and minor device number of the device with the corrupt file system. This error means that some file is claimed to use a block which is not within the limits of the file system on which the file exists. You will probably have to repair this file system.

bad count on d/d

This also indicates a corrupt file system; it means that the count of free blocks or free i-nodes on the file system is bad. Again, repair is called for.

no space on d/d

This indicates that the free space on the file system on the device in question has been exhausted. People may have lost parts of their files if they were writing them out from the editor; this is not recoverable. The best course of action is to use "/etc/wall" to send a warning message to all users that they should not create any files on or copy any files to that file system and urge people to remove files from that file system.

Out of inodes on d/d

This indicates that the free space in the i-list of the file system on the device in question has been exhausted. The same comments apply as with the "no space" message.

no file

This indicates that a program tried to open a file, but there weren't enough slots in the system "open file" table to accomodate it. The best course is to warn users with "/etc/wall" if this error repeatedly occurs, and to increase the size of the "open file" table.

Inode table overflow

This indicates that a program tried to use a file, but there weren't enough slots in the system "in-core inode" table to accomodate it. Again, warn users if this repeatedly occurs, and increase the size of the "in-core inode" table.

panic: reason

This indicates an error so serious that the operating system could not continue to run. The machine should be halted, and the reason noted. The possible reason's are:

"out of swap space"

This indicates that the space available on the swapping area of disk space for programs swapped out of main memory has been exhausted. Either more swap space should be found or the maximum number of processes allowed on the system should be reduced.

"out of text"

This indicates that the system tried to execute a program whose executable code portion could be shared between multiple users using that program, but there weren't enough slots in the system "shared text" table to record that this program was in use. You have to increase the size of the "shared text" table for your system.

"swap error"

This indicates that an I/O error occurred in the process of swapping a program out to the swap area or swapping it in to main memory. Before this message, an I/O error message should have been printed on the system console. If this problem recurs, have a customer engineer look at the drive which has the swap area on it.

"no clock"

This indicates that UNIX was unable to start the hardware clock on the machine. If such a clock is installed, this indicates hardware dificulties.

"parity"

This indicates a main memory parity error; this is a hardware failure.

"(other)"

Other "panics" indicate either a software problem in the operating system or a hardware problem.

APPENDIX B

Archive and Library Maintainer

ar option [posname] archive_file
   [file1...]

options

d delete files from lib

r replace files in lib

t print files in lib

x extract files from lib

v verbose

c create lib

Build Special Files

/etc/mknod name [c] [b] major minor

-c file is character file

-b file is block file

major minor specific driver

Change Group

chgrp group file...

Change Mode

chmod option file...

options

4000 execution mode user

2000 execution mode group

0400 read permission

0200 write permission

0100 execute permission

0070 group read,write,execute permission

0007 all others

Change Owner

chown owner file...

Clear i-nodes

clri filesystem i-number...

Compare Two Files

comm [-[123]] file1 file2

123 represent columns displayed

Compare Two Files

cmp [-l][-s] file1 file2

-l provide complete diff table

-s return code based on results

Concatenate Files

cat [-u] [file1...]

-u specify block size other

Construct a File System

/etc/mkfs [filesystem] [block count]

Convert and Copy a File

dd [option-value]...

options

if= input file

of= output file

bs=n set both ip/op block size

skip=n skip n ip records

files=n compy n files from tape

seek=n seek n rec's

count=n compy only n ip rec's

conv=

ascii EBCDIC to ASCII

ebcdic ASCII to EBCDIC

lcase map to lower case

ucase map to upper case

Copy Files

cp file1 file2

or

cp file1...filen directory

Determine File Type

file filename

le1...filen directory

Diff Between Versions of a File

diff3 [-ex3] file1 file2 file3

-e output accepted by editor

-x3 only differences in file3

Differences Between Two Files

diff [-efbh] file1 file2

-e produces editor commands

-b ignore trailing blanks and tabs

-f produce script of diff's

-h faster check

Disk Free Space

df [file system]

Dismount a File System

/etc/umount filesystem

Echo Argument

echo [-n] [arg]...

-n eliminate new lines

Directory Consistency Check

dcheck [-i numbers] [filesystem]

numbers obtained from itself or icheck

Storage Consistency Check

icheck [-s] [-b numbers] [filesystem]

-s reconstruct new free list

-b issue error when block #found

Find Pattern Matches in Files

grep [option]... expression [file]

options

-v print lines not matching

-n line preceded by its line number

-y match lower case letters to upper

Generate Names from i-numbers

ncheck [-i numbers] [-a] [-s]
    [filesystem]

-i produces path names

-s produces path's for special files

Get Terminal Name

tty

Incremental File System Dump

dump [option [argument...] filesystem]

options

f place dump on next arg file

u after completing,write date

0-9 dump level

s specify size of tape

d specify density in "BPI"

Incremental File System Restore

restor option [argument...]

options

f specify specific tape

r or R specify filesystem

x extract each named file

t prints date

y size of tape

List the Contents of a Directory

ls [-option...] name...

options

l long list

t sort by time

a list all entries(. and ..)

d status of named directory

Mount a File System

/etc/mount [filesystem [-r]]

-r mount as read only

Move Files

mv file1 file2

or

mv directory1 directory2

or

mv file1...filen directory2

Octal Dump

od [-bcdox] file [[+offset[.][b]]

c interpreted in ASCII

d interpreted in decimal

o interpreted in octal

x interpreted in hex

Permit or Deny Messages

mesg [n] [y]

Pipe Fitting

tee [options] [file]...

options

-i ignores interrupts

-a append output to file

Print and Set Date

date [yymmddhhmm[.ss]]

Print Calendar

cal [month] year

Print File

pr [option]... [file]...

options

-n n column output

+n start print nth page

-h next arg as page header

-wn width of page

-ln length of page

Process Status

ps [option...] [namelist]

options

a list all process from terminals

x list all process (system)

l long list

Remove Files

rm [options] file...

options

-f forse all files to be deleted

-r delete all files & subdir's

-i interactive delete

Report Repeated Lines in a File

uniq [-options [+n] [-n]] [input] [output]

options

u lines not repeated are output

d only repeated lines are output

Run a Command at Low Priority

nice [-number] command [arguments]

number 1-20 with 20 lowest priority

Sending and Receiving Mail

mail [login name]...

Setting a Terminal

stty [option...]

Setting the Terminal Tabs

tabs [-n] [terminal]

-n left margin not indented

Sort or Merge Files

sort [-option...] [+pos1 [-pos2]]...

[-o name] [-T directory] [name]...

options

b ignore leading blanks

f upper lower case letters

m merge

n sorted by arithmetic value

o output file

u eliminate duplicates

Split a File into Pieces

split [-n] [file [name]]

-n no. lines to be placed in output

Substitute User ID Temporarily

su [userid]

Suspend Execution for an Interval

sleep time

time is in seconds

Table of Contents for Archive Files

ranlib [archive file....]

Tape Archiver

tar [option] [name]

options

r names written on end of tape

x names are extracted from tape

t list names

u added to tape if not there

0,...,7 select tape drive

v print names

b blocking factor

Terminate a Process

kill [-option] processid...

option = signal number

Update the Super Block

sync

Who is on the System

who [who-file] [am i]

Word Count

wc [-lwc] [file....]

l count number lines

w count number words

c count number characters

Working Directory Name

pwd

Write to all Users

wall

Write to Another User

write user [ttyname]

Find Files

find pathname... option...

option

-name filename

-mtime n T if modified in n days

-print prints current pathname

Summarize Disk Usage

du [-s] [-a] [name...]

-s provide only grand total

-a generate entry for each file

APPENDIX C

Chapter Two

(1) Request it from the system administrator.

(2) It's your choise, however it should be short and easy to remember.

(3) The password should be sex or more characters. It can be shorter if complex(i.e., invisible and special characters).

(4) Ask the system administrator to remove it.

(5) One or more blanks

(6) Depress the return kcy.

(7) Generally responds with the prompt sign "$".

(8) "$"

(9) Enter the character "#" immediatly after the bad character.

(10) You can kill it by use of the "@" character.

Chapter Three

(1) a) returns the message "?filename". b) returns the message "n" where n = size of file in bytes

(2) When the append mode is invoked, you are positioned just after the line you where at when append was invoked.

(3) You must be on a new line and then enter the character ".".

(4) a) append   a(r)

.(r)

add new text

text is added after current position

b) insert i(r)

.(r)

insert new text

text is inserted before current position

c) change c(r)

.(r)

change(replace) existing lines of text

text is changed at current position

d) delete d(r)

nothing required

delete current line of text

line of text is deleted at current position

e) print p(r)

nothing required

delete current line of text

line of text is deleted at current position

(5) Using the substitute command. s/oldtext/newtext/

(6) Use the "w" commmand. Ed will respond with the number of characters written.

(7) The quit command "q".

(8) With the command "1,$p"

(9) The editor will display the character "?".

(10) $– is determined by context and means either (1) the end of a line, or (2) the end of the file.

^– This character indicates the beginning of a line of text.

* – This means any number of consecutive occurences of the same character.

g – When used with commands such as substitute, it refers to global. When in front of the command it is global for that line of text, and when it appears at the end of the command, its range is over the entire file or the range specified.

(11) a) print line number currently positioned at.

    b) print line just before current line positioned at.

    c) print line just after current line positioned at

    d) print current line positioned at.

    e) replace lines 1,2,3 with one line "new line".

    f) delete current line positioned at plus next 3 lines.

    g) find first occurrance of the text "The"

    h) Add the text "the" to the beginning of the line currently positioned at.

    i) write the complete file (lines 1 to the end) out to a new file named "newfile"

    j) add the character "$" to the end of the current line of text.

    k) replace all strings "you" in the current line with the text "I".

    l) replace all strings "I" in the file with the text "you".

Chapter Four

(1) In your root directory(i.e., if your login name is "dick", you would probalbly be in the directory ".../dick".

(2) Limits are what iis set by the system administrator. You can continue creating subdirectors and files until the system complaines.

(3) Hierarchical file system.

(4) Use the command "pwd".

(5) a) list subdirectories and files within the current directory.

    b) change to another directory.

    c) make a new directory.

    d) remove an existing directory.

    e) remove files.

(6) Use the "ls -l" command. All directories will start with "drw....",and all files will start with "-rw....".

(7) Owner(login name), group, and all others.

(8)   a) positioned at user root "dick"

     b) positioned at dick/A/A1

     c) positioned at dick/A/A2

     d) positioned at dick/B

     e) removed directory B1

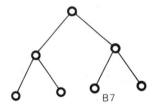

B7

     f) error can't remove directory A1(positioned incorrectly)

     g) dick/B

     h) the new structure looks as:

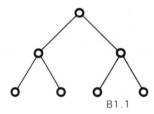

B1.1

Chapter Five

(1)   The output from the following commands is:

a)   1 1 1 1 1 1
         1 1 1 1 1 1
         2 2 2 2 2 2
         2 2 2 2 2 2

b) $ – data is in file4

c)   – The system will wait for input from your terminal and place it in the file "file4"

(2) The file "file1" is spooled to the printer and waits for its turn to be printed. UNIX gives control back and issues the prompt "$" as soon as the file has been queued for printing.

(3) It provides for limited formation of your text such as page numbers and headers. It does not direct the output to a given printer, but to the standard output.

(4) a) change directory to A and copy file F1 to the directory B providing the same file name "F1".

b) Change directory to user root dick and copy file F2 from directory A to directory B changing the file name to FA.

c) Copy all files in directory A to directory B keeping all file names the same. Directory A will be unchanged.

d) Move all files in directory B to directory C and when complete, B will be an empty directory.

e) Move file FA from directory C to directory B changing its name to F1.

(5) The owner and group of a file enjoy the read/write protections. Thus protection can allow an owner or a group the right to read and/or write a file.

(6) a) read/write/execute for owner, read/execute for group and others

-rwxr-x-r-x

b) read/write for owner and group, read only for all others

-rw-rw-r–

c) read/write/execute only for owner

-rwx–

d) read/write for owner, read only for group and others

-rw-r–r–

Chapter Six

(1) Standard input/output is used. It accepts input from the users terminal and putputs text back to the users terminal.

(2) The character ">" is used to direct data from a command to a new file. In this case if the file already existed, the data would have been replaced with the new data. If the existing data in an existing file was to be saved, and the new data concatenated to it, the character ">>" is used.

(3) The use of the special characters "<" and "<<".

(4) A process is a computer function performing a single task.

(5) Yes; by use of the special character "&" which is attached to the end of your command.

(6) Yes; by use of the special character "fi" placed between the command passing the data and the command receiving the data.

(7) They are metacharacters and are used for creating patterns that help locate files and directory names. The first "*" means any number of characters and the "?" means any single character in that position.

(8) Creates a pattern that will select only those names starting with a letter "a,b,c,d,...,z". The remainder of the name can be anything.

Chapter Seven

Communications

(1) Yes; the only limit is that they must have a legal login name.

(2) Yes; the mail will be dated and time stamped and will remain there until you view it.

(3) When you login or anytime after that you may enter "mail" and see if you have mail.

(4) Yes; using the command "wall".

(5) The message is sent as soon as you depress the control-d on your terminal and it's received immediatly.

(6) You can write to anyone who is currently logged in and has not denied you permission by use of the mesg command.

Information Handling

(1) dd if=mt0 conv=ascii

(2) diff -e file1 file2

(3) grep Syntax *

(4) a) produce a line, word, and character count for the file "file1".

b) split the file "file1" into 10 equal parts placing the results in Faa , Fab , ...,Faj.

c) Sort the file "file1" in reverse order and place the output in the file "file2".

Running Programs

(1) Provides a "echo" of the ext selected by you (arguments to the command echo). Generally used to create a trace (or flow) of multiple commands.

command echo). Generally used to create a trace (or flow) of multiple commands.

(2) kill -9 102 use the "ps" command

(3) "nice" where the argument can be 1 to 20 with 20 being the lowest priority.

Statistics

(1) issue the "pwd" command.

(2) df /dev/usr

(3) date

(4) who am i

(5) ps a

(6) cal 1981 – don't put 81 for 1981, because it will give you the year 81.

Terminals

(1) stty 1200 > /dev/tty3 – notice that you have to direct the output because it is not your terminal.

(2) Most printers can skip over tabs faster then over blanks. Thus the printer should print faster.

(3)   tabs 1620

Chapter Eight

(1)   A shell file is exactly the same as any other file except that it contains
      UNIX and/or ED commands that can be executed. Its value is that it
      requires no programming experience and yet it can perform tasks that
      would otherwise require programming experience.

(2)   9 arguments are allowed. The values may be $1, $2, ... , $9.

(3)   An example of nested procedures would be where procedure A invoked
      procedure B.

(4) $MAIL, $HOME, $PATH are special variables.

Chapter Nine

(1)   Two privileged users - superuser and bin. The superuser has access
      to everything, protections do not have any affect. The bin user has
      control over the directories /bin and /usr/bin.

(2)   a) edit the password file "/etc/passwd"

      b) add new user to end of password file.

      c) make a directory for the user.

      d) change the owner of the directory to that of the new user

      e) set the priorities if any.

(3)   Use the "wall" command.

(4)   use the "ps axl" command.

(5)   after a power failure

(6)   use df /dev/filesystem

      or

      icheck /dev/filesystem

(7)   Place the commands in the file /etc/rc.

(8)   By editing the /etc/ttys file. The first chatacter is 0 or 1 where 0 =
      deactivate and 1 = activate. You must bring the system down to a
      simgle user status after changing the ttys file and then bring it back
      up to multi user.

(9) An i-number is the number of an i-node(or index), where the i-number of a file may be thought of as the system's internal name or identifier for a file.

Backup and Maintenance

(1) a) icheck - Used to examine a file system by checking for consistency for both the free block list and for the sued blocks. b) ncheck - Provides the pathnames associated with i-numbers. c) clri - Primary purpose of this command is to remove a file which doesn't appear in a directory or for removing i-nodes.

(2) The files on a file system (other then the root file system) cannot be accessed by users until the file system is mounted

(3) Become the superuser by issuing the command "su" or login as the owner of those files.

(4) The primary purpose of the dump command is to create a backup in case of computer failure, whereas tar is used for selective dumps that can be easily restored.

APPENDIX D

(1) D. M. Ritchie and K. Thompson, "The UNIX Time-Sharing System," Comm. ACM, Vol. 17, No. 7, July 1974, pp.365-375.

(2) D. M. Ritchie, "UNIX Time-Sharing System: A Retrospective," Bell System Technical J., Vol. 57, No. 6, Oct. 1978, pp. 1947-1969.

(3) D. M. Ritchie, S. C. Johnson, M. E. Lesk, and B. W. Kernighan, "UNIX Time-Sharing System: The C Programming Language," Bell System Technical J., Vol. 57, No. 6, Oct. 1978, pp. 1991-2019.

(4) B. W. Kernighan and D. M. Ritchie, The C Programming Language, Prentice-Hall, Englewood Cliffs, N.J., 1978.

(5) K. Thompson, "The UNIX Command Language," in Structured Programming – Infotech State of the Art Report, Infotech International Ltd., Berkshire, England, Mar. 1975, pp.375-384.

(6) S. R. Bourne, "An Introduction to the UNIX Shell," Bell System Technical J., Vol. 57, No. 6, Oct. 1978, pp.2792-2822.

(7) S. C. Johnson and D. M. Ritchie, "UNIX Time-Sharing System: Portability of C Programs and the UNIX System," Bell System Technical J., Vol. 57, No. 6, Oct. 1978, pp.2021-2048.

(8) B. W. Kernighan and J. R. Mashey, "The UNIX Programming Environment," Software–Practice & Experience, Vol. 9, No. 1, January 1979.

(9) Richard Miller, "UNIX–A Portable Operating System?" Operating Systems Rev., Vol. 12, No. 3, July 1978, pp.32-37.

(10) T. A. Dollotta and J. R. Mashey, "An Introduction to the Programmer's Workbench," Proc. 2nd Int'l Conf. Software Eng., Oct. 1976, pp. 164-168.

(11) E. L. Ivie, "The Programmer's Workbench–A Machine for Software Development," Comm. ACM, Vol. 20, No. 10, Oct. 1977, pp.746-753.

(12) J. Lions, "Experiences with the UNIX Time-Sharing System,"

Software–Practice & Experience, Vol. 9, No. 9, September 1979.

(13) T. A. Dolotta, R. C. Haight, and J. R. Mashey, "UNIX Time-Sharing System: The Programmer's Workbench," Bell System Technical J., Vol. 57, No. 6, Oct. 1978, pp. 2177-2200.

(14) J. R. Mashey, "Using a Command Language as a High-Level Programming Language," Proc. 2nd Int'l Conf. Software Eng., Oct. 1976, pp. 169-176.

(15) T. A. Dolotta and J. R. Mashey, "Using a Command Language as the Primary Programming Tool," in Command Language Directions: Proc. 79 IFIP Working Conf. Command Languages, D. Beech, ed., North-Holland, Amsterdam, The Netherlands, 1980.

(16) D. M. Harland, "High Speed Data Acquisition:Running a Realtime Process and a Time-Shared System (UNIX) Concurrently," Software–Practice & Experience, Vol. 10, No. 4, April 1980.

(17) D. M. Ritchie, "The Evolution of the UNIX Time-Sharing System," Proc. Symp. Language Design and Programming Methodology, Sidney, Australia, 1979.

(18) E. Yourdon and L. L. Constantine, Structured Design, Yourdon Press, London, 1975.

(19) M. A. Jackson, Principles of Program Design, Academic Press, London, 1975.

(20) F. T. Baker, "Structured Programming in the Production Programming Environment," Proc. Int'l Conf. Reliable Software, 1975, pp. 172-185.

(21) M. J. Rochkind, "The Source Code Control System," IEEE Trans. Software Eng., Vol. SE-1, No. 4, Dec. 1975, pp. 364-370.

(22) A. L. Glasser, "The Evolution of a Source Code Control System," SICSOFT, Vol. 3, No. 5, Nov. 1978, pp. 121-125.

(23) S. I. Fieldman, "MAKE–A Program for Maintaining Computer Programs," UNIX Programmer's Manual, Vol. 9, Apr. 1979, pp. 255-265.

(24) D. J. Pearson, "The Use and Abuse of a Software Engineering System," AFIPS Conf. Proc., 1979 NCC, pp. 1029-1035.

(25) D. Teichroew and E. A. Hershey III, "PLS/PSA: A Computer-Aided

Technique for Structured Documentation and Analysis of Information Processing Systems," IEEE Trans. Software Eng., Vol. SE-3, No. 1, Jan. 1977, pp. 42-48.

(26) W. Teitelman, INTERLISP Reference Manual, Xerox Corp. Palo Alto Research Center, Palo Alto, Calif., Dec. 1978.

(27) W. Teitelman, "A Display Oriented Programmer's Assistant," CSL 77-3, Xerox Corp. Palo Alto Research Center, Palo Alto, Calif., Mar. 1977.

(28) A. Kay and A. Goldberg, "Personal Dynamic Media," Computer, Mar. 1977, pp. 31-41.

(29) B. W. Kernighan and P. J. Plauger, Software Tools, Addison-Wesley, Reading, Mass., 1976.

(30) D. E. Hall, D. K. Scherrer, and J. S. Sventek, "A Virtual Operating System," Comm. ACM, Vol. 23, No. 9, Sept. 1980, pp. 495-502.

(31) C. R. Snow, "The Software Tools Project," Software–Practice & Experience, Vol. 8, No. 5, Sept.-Oct. 1978.

(32) P. H. Enslow, Jr., Portability of Large Cobol Programs: The Cobol Programmer's Workbench, Georgia Institute of Technology, Atlanta, Ga., Sept. 1979.

(33) J. P. L. Woodward, "Applications for Multilevel Secure Operating Systems," AFIPS Conf. Proc., 1979 NCC, June 1979, pp. 319-328.

(34) G. J. Popek et al., "UCLA Secure UNIX," AFIPS Conf. Proc., 1979 NCC, June 1979, pp. 355-364.

(35) E. J. McCauley and P. J. Drongowski, "KSOS–The Design of a Secure Operating System," AFIPS Conf. Proc., 1979 NCC, June 1979, pp. 345-353.

(36) E. J. McCauley, G. L. Barksdale, and J. Holden, "Software Development Using a Development Support Machine," ADA Environment Workshop, DoD High Order Language Working Group, Nov. 1979, pp. 1-9.

(37) M. Risenberg, "Software Costs Can Be Tamed, Developers Told," Computerworld, Jan. 29, 1980, pp. 1-8.

(38) J. E. Stockenberg and D. Taffs, "Software Test Bed Support Under PWB/UNIX," ADA Environment Workshop, DoD High Order

Language Working Group, Nov. 1979, pp. 10-26.

(39) R. A. Allshouse, D. T. McClellan, E. G. Prine and C. P. Rolla, "CSDP as an ADA Environment," ADA Environment Workshop, DoD High Order Language Working Group, No. 1979, pp. 113-125.

(40) P. Wegner, "The ADA Language and Environment," Proc. Electro/80, Western Periodicals Co., North Hollywood, Calif., May 1980.

(41) R. A. Robinson and E. A. Krzysiak, "An Integrated Support Software Network Using NSW Technology," AFIPS Conf. Proc., 1980 NCC, May 1980, pp. 671-676.

(42) A. B. Barak and A. Shapir, "UNIX with Satellite Processors," Software–Practice & Experience, Vol. 10, No. 5, May 1980.

(43) P.Brinch Hansen, "Sructured multiprogramming," Prentice-Hall, Inc., Englewood Cliffs, N.J., 1978.

(44) H. Lycklama and C. Christensen, "A minicomputer satellite processor system," The Bell System Tech. Journal, 57, 6, part 2, 2103-2113 (1978)

(45) K. Thompson and D. M. Ritchie, UNIX Programmer's Manual, 6th edn., Bell Telephone Lab., Murray Hill, N. J., 1975.

(46) J. Lions, "The UNIX Operating System," Commentary, Bell Telephone Laboratories, Murray Hill, N. J., 1977.

(47) W. N. Joy, S. L. Graham and C. B. Haley, "UNIX Pascal User's Manual," Department of Electrical Engineering and Computer Science, University of California, Berkeley, 1977.

(48) J. Larmouth, "Scheduling for a share of the machine," Software–Practice and Experience, 5, 29-49 (1974).

(49) J. Lions, "An operation system case study," Operating Systems Review, 12, No. 3, 46-53 (1978).

APPENDIX E